HARDHAT DAYS

HARDHAT DAYS

MY RE-EDUCATION IN SEATTLE'S SHIPYARDS

MIKE NOLAN

Basalt Books
Pullman, Washington

Basalt Books
PO Box 645610
Pullman, Washington 99164-5610
Phone: 800-354-7360
Email: basalt.books@wsu.edu
Website: basaltbooks.wsu.edu

First printing 2025

Basalt Books is an imprint of Washington State University Press.

While this story is nonfiction, many names have been changed to protect the privacy of the individuals.

The Washington State University Pullman campus is located on the homelands of the Niimíipuu (Nez Perce) Tribe and the Palus people. We acknowledge their presence here since time immemorial and recognize their continuing connection to the land, to the water, and to their ancestors. WSU Press is committed to publishing works that foster a deeper understanding of the Pacific Northwest and the contributions of its Native peoples.

Interior design by Tracy Randall
Cover design by Noah Van Soest.
Cover image is of the author during the period covered in this memoir.

Dedication

To Jay, Lucy, and Madeline for their ongoing encouragement and support.

And to Ann, for her love, wisdom, patience and guidance.

CONTENTS

CHAPTER 1

On the day my life was going to end, Washington fixed me with his implacable stare and growled, "Are you the one gonna blast that son of a bitch?" The foreman's features were carved in stone. He jerked his thumb over his shoulder. "We got a job to do here."

Standing next to him on the wooden pier, I held Washington's gaze without betraying my thoughts. *I hate the fat bastard, but…*as much as I couldn't stand the foreman, I still wanted to measure up in his eyes. I still *needed* to measure up.

Washington and I turned to face three thousand tons of haze-gray steel floating in the water. The USS *Roark*, a sleek four-hundred-foot-long Navy frigate, outlined against a cloudless blue Seattle sky. The *Roark*'s superstructure and tower rose above us, gigantic and imposing.

"Sure, I can handle it." Searching the foreman's face, I hoped I looked as confident as I was trying to sound.

Now that he had the upper hand, Washington reverted to form, folding his arms and shifting his imposing bulk my way. The foreman was good at that: he could shove people around with his oversized body *and* with his words. "I'm serious—serious as a heart attack," was one of his favorite lines.

I was not alone in my contempt for Washington, but as the new guy, and being unsure of myself, I cared about his opinion of my work. After laboring as a sandblaster in the shipyard for a few months, I believed I possessed the skills to do this job. I wanted to convince Washington, too.

A light breeze whistled through the metal rigging overhead, and my gaze wandered up along the superstructure and tower, all the way to the crow's nest, a hundred feet in the sky. That's where I'd begin blasting.

Washington caught my gaze. "That crow's nest is nothin' but a platform with a railing runnin' round it," he said. "No sweat blasting once you're up there."

Was that supposed to reassure me? Make the job look simple? *That's easy for you to say.* I maintained the mask. "No problem," I said. *He's trying to make it sound like anyone could blast this.*

The morning felt warm for spring, with enough sunshine to heat the creosote dock and pilings where we stood. The marine alchemy of softened tar and salty sea air created one of the few pleasant smells in the shipyard, and it drifted over the placid surface of Elliott Bay, the still water at odds with what lay ahead for me.

Washington let out a long breath. "Okay then, let's do it. Get suited up." In a rare moment of helpfulness, the foreman looked at me and added, "Richards is running the sand pot over on the fantail. I'll tell him you're getting ready." Extending himself meant only one thing: Washington was damn relieved to hand this job off to someone. I was really glad it was me.

There were a half-dozen other sandblasters at Lockheed Shipyard on Harbor Island, all of them far more qualified than me. I was the youngest and least senior, with the next guy having at least ten years' experience on me. I knew Washington was desperate to get someone to do this particular job after overhearing a conversation he had with a more senior blaster, who'd replied, "Now why would I wanna drag my ass up that tower? Ask the kid to do it...hell, Nolan *wants* the work."

That much was true. The kid—me—was the guy who craved more experience. I wanted to run with the old pros, to make sandblasting look easy the way they did, but I knew that wouldn't happen overnight. The best I could hope for was to blast everything I could get my hands on, gaining experience and busting my ass doing it, then hope down the road I'd hear something like "You gotta give the kid credit..."

Thirty minutes later, I scaled the superstructure and tower ladders, hand over hand, in a harness and full sandblasting gear. The morning continued to warm, and it felt ten degrees hotter inside the heavy black rubber sandblaster's hood I was wearing. Even with an air hose blowing full blast in my face, sweat rolled down the back of my head and neck as I climbed. The two-by-four-inch plate-glass window on the face of my hood fogged up, creating gauzy tunnel vision. After ascending to the crow's nest and crawling through the trapdoor, I pulled myself onto the metal deck, panting. *I haven't even started blasting and I'm already winded.* The air stream whistled past my face and cleared the plate glass as I swiveled my head around to take in the view. *Jesus, I'm up high.*

Out beyond the shipyard, past Elliott Bay, the Seattle skyscrapers gleamed silver and gray in the midmorning sun. Beyond downtown, the sprawl of the city carpeted the hillsides. And farther out...*Is that Bellevue?* The Cascade Mountain Range hemmed the landscape in, with its mammoth jewel, Mount Rainier, dominating in the south.

Time to get to work. I waved to the sand pot tender, Richards, signaling to fire me up. Raising the steel nozzle over my head and bending the hose in an arc against my shoulder, I pressed the trigger. The deafening rush of sand created a billowing black cloud of grit that enveloped the crow's nest. The sandstorm surrounding me was disorienting and at the same time soothing, creating a surreal world of my own.

Everything above the superstructure of the ship was aluminum and, being softer than steel, required only a light, quick blast. *Knock this sucker out…show that oversized bastard Washington you've got what it takes.* Working a little too fast along the railing, I turned to blast the first post, with both hands on the hose. I took a step across the deck of the crow's nest to continue along the railing, but my foot didn't touch anything. No resistance. Open space. The deck wasn't there.

"OH GOD! OH GOD! OH GOD!"

I'm in the air, falling through the open trapdoor—in free fall—a hundred feet up. I'm going to splatter on the ship's deck.

My perceptions became elastic, and everything seemed to slow down. The moment stretched out long enough for me to watch the metal deck pass by. A steady stream of sand sprayed out in front of me from the hose I still clutched.

An incredible jolt hammered my left side and lower back. "*AAAAGH,*" I yelled. My neck whiplashed; my arms and legs ricocheted down and then upward in opposition to the blow while the hose flew out of my hands, flaying wildly. A second later my body stabilized, and I hung in the air sideways, six feet below the crow's nest.

I dangled from the nylon strap of my safety harness like a perpendicular puppet on a string, realizing I had automatically clipped the harness to the railing without even thinking about it. *Jesus fucking Christ.* The unconscious *click* of the harness carabiner saved my life.

Slowly twisting in the gentle breeze, my body defined a lazy arc. The tower and ladder came back into view through my plate-glass window. *God, my side hurts.* I reached out with both hands for the reassuring touch of the aluminum railing, grabbed a rung, and reoriented myself. *Head up, feet down.* My side and back were on fire.

I lined my body up with the ladder and got one foot on a rung. Far below my boots, the upturned faces of a dozen workers—the foreman included—gazed back at me, uncharacteristically frozen in what would normally be a chaotic work day. On the fantail the pot tender, Richards, stared too, open mouthed. He'd had the presence of mind to cut the pressure at the sand pot, and the blasting hose now hung flaccid, swaying by my side.

Hand over hand, I climbed back into the crow's nest, pulled up the sandblasting hose behind me, and closed the metal trapdoor. *Here I am trying to impress the foreman, but if I don't slow down and watch what the hell I'm doing, I'll kill myself. That's how stupid I'm being right now.*

Ignoring the workers below, I made a lasso motion to Richards, indicating I was ready to start again. He reached down and, grabbing a lever, charged the hose, and I resumed blasting where I left off.

Surprisingly, it took only a few minutes to overcome the shock of impending death and return to the rhythm of work, although every time I took a tentative step, my eyes cut to the trapdoor, now closed, until I muttered an exasperated "I shut it" out loud inside my hood. I blasted the metal grating deck, then opened the trap door back up and descended a few steps, slapping the harness carabiner on the ladder and blasting underneath the crow's nest. I continued to work my way down the tower to the superstructure until Richards cut the pressure two hours later, letting me know it was time to knock off for lunch.

After climbing down the superstructure to the deck, I removed my hood and stripped off my rain gear, finally tearing away the duct-taped cuffs and taking off my jacket. My side and back throbbed. Pulling up my shirt, I stared at an angry purple bruise that circled halfway around my waist.

I groaned and gazed out across Elliott Bay. The stark contrast between city and sky made downtown Seattle look like a Hollywood prop: an unreal, one-dimensional cutout framed against a brilliant, solid blue background. *I'm okay*, I reassured myself, looking out at the city I called home. That familiar scene always made me feel good, in a "glad to be alive" way. Realizing my sentimental cliché, I laughed—which made my side hurt worse—and walked toward the fantail, where I ran into Washington.

"So…" He glanced at me, then cut his eyes back to the tower. "You can knock out the rest of the sandblasting after lunch, right?" *Pure Washington.*

"I'm fine," I said, turning away from the foreman, then hollered over my shoulder, "Don't worry…it'll get done," adding under my breath, "as long as I clip that fucking safety harness." I walked the rest of the way to the fantail.

Richards was stooped over the sand pot, keeping busy with the valves. Seeing me, he straightened up and reached out for my shoulder. This was the man who got me here, the person I owed my job to, the one who'd felt sorry for me back when I was desperate and needed a break. At that time, Richards had taken me under his wing and taught me about sandblasting, becoming my mentor. Richards' opinion mattered way more to me than Washington's, and I knew I had let him down.

I wasn't greeted with Richards's usual smile. I felt like I was back in high school, waiting in the principal's office, guilty over some transgression and preparing for a well-deserved ass chewing. We stood and stared at each other, then his eyes narrowed and he said in a serious tone, "No more dancing up there, Nolan."

"No more dancing," I repeated, my words even, my eyes unblinking.

Richards held my gaze long enough to make me sweat, then his expression softened, and he went back to the Richards I was accustomed to. He brought his face close to mine and said in a low, steady voice, "Seriously, you watch yourself, Nolan." His focus returned to the sand pot, and he casually added over his shoulder, "Ain't no job worth your life, you know what I mean?"

I jammed my hands into my coverall pockets, looked away, and nodded in agreement, knowing I had disappointed him. "You're right," I said, barely audible. "I was on the goddamned razor's edge." The shipyard whistle, high pitched and shrill, broke the spell.

Richards and I silently walked the length of the main deck to the broad aluminum gangway, gradually becoming part of the human current of a hundred workers leaving the ship for lunch. Richards headed for the vending machines while I washed up in the locker room, then grabbed my lunch pail and sat down with the group of guys I always ate with: grizzled, boisterous hard-hat types unwinding for thirty minutes.

"Those Mariners are looking good in spring training," someone said.

"Wait till the season starts," someone else laughed, "then they'll disappoint you."

I breathed a sigh of relief, realizing none of the men at my table had witnessed my sandblasting fiasco. The last thing I wanted was to spend my lunch break explaining why I'd been stupid enough to end up hanging sideways from the crow's nest like a brainless marionette. I stared into the distance and took a bite of sandwich while the banter became a monotone in the background. My mind drifted away and my eyes glazed over, until the world tilted and my body fell through the trapdoor all over again. That was the closest I'd come to death.

Richards was right: I had to watch myself. People get hurt in the shipyard all the time. There's nothing routine about heavy construction; it requires patience and focus, and today I lacked both, trying to show off for the foreman. Mentally crossing off one of my nine lives, I cleared my throat and took another bite of sandwich, willing my attention back to the Mariners and spring training.

The whistle blew, signaling the end of lunch, and the guys around me drained their coffee cups. I stood slowly and winced, once again sensitive to my side. Lunch pails were stashed, locker doors slammed. Taking my time, I gingerly descended the creaky wooden staircase, favoring my right side while trying not to show it.

Halfway down the stairs I heard a familiar voice behind me. My friend Lamar—a light-skinned Black man with almond-shaped eyes and a pencil-thin mustache—caught up to me. He put his hand on my shoulder, saying in his singsong voice, "Yo, Master Blaster. That couldn't a been you up there—was it?—dangling from the crow's nest of the *Roark* this morning?"

Terrific...so Lamar had seen me. I wasn't the master of *anything* at the moment, let alone blasting, so all I could manage was "Yeah, that was me." I avoided his gaze and continued down the steps.

Lamar kept pace with me. "That was some pretty fancy sandblasting..." His eyes danced as a cigarette bobbed up and down from his lips. "Kinda like, you know, in the circus."

"Well, what can I say?" I kept my chin up and tried to sound cool. "That's what sandblasters do."

Lamar was having none of it. He knew better. "Yeah, right." Then his grin widened. "That, and kill themselves."

I stopped. Lamar patted my shoulder as he stepped down past me.

"That's okay," he said, nodding. "You almost killed yourself up there, an' you still kept on workin'. But you take care, Brother Nols. We wanna keep you around." When he got to the bottom of the stairs, Lamar turned around and laughed. "We gotta have us at least *one* white sandblaster in this shipyard, ya know, even if he really wants to be an ac-ro-bat."

Now I started to laugh, nodding and tipping my hard hat. What else was there to do? With a grin on my face, I said, "Right on, Lamar." I had to give my friend credit: whatever the circumstances, even life or death, Lamar could put me in a good mood.

I walked across the yard in the direction of the *Roark*, hands in my pockets and eyes fixed on the tower. Had I convinced Washington that morning I had the chops to make it as a sandblaster? Probably not.

I shrugged. *Who cares?* At least Lamar thinks I have what it takes.

As I got back to work, I tried *not* to think of the spectacle of me dangling from the crow's nest. The hell with it. It wasn't any worse than the last time I was humiliated: being accosted by a cop at three in the morning while sleeping on the sidewalk in the Central District.

CHAPTER 2

(six months earlier)

It was well after midnight in the Central District, and the businesses along Twenty-Third and East Madison were closed, except for the Honeysuckle Tavern: it was still going strong, even at this hour. I had totally struck out job hunting, and now tried to make myself comfortable leaning against the door of the Ship Scalers Union Hall, my way of assuring I'd be the first person in line for the early morning job call.

A little after two, tavern barflies emptied into the street, trying to find their cars, and by two thirty, East Madison was completely deserted, dark and silent. I sat with my back against the union hall door, a blanket over my shoulders, my eyelids growing heavy. That's the last thing I remember before the stillness was shattered with "You can't sleep here! You can't sleep on the sidewalk!"

I jumped, startled by the booming voice, eyes now wide open. The problem was, I couldn't see anything because of the oversized flashlight directly in front of my face.

"Let's go," the voice commanded, as the flashlight waived. I blinked a couple times and recognized the metallic glint on some sort of suit on the other side of the light. "*I said let's go*," the voice repeated, and I recognized the uniform of a Seattle Police officer.

I disentangled myself from the blanket and cleared my throat. "I'm trying to get a job," I managed to get out, half sitting up. "What I mean is"—I cleared my throat again—"I'm trying to get in line for a job call."

The officer took a step back and scanned his light over my body, then put it back in my face. It was impossible to see around this bulky guy towering over me.

I struggled to my feet. "The line, ah, what I mean is"—I took a deep breath—"there's a call for jobs here at the union hall in the morning, and I've lined up twice already, but I haven't been far enough in line to get the call." I realized I was talking too fast. "I just wanna get a job," I said, slowing down, "so this time I'm going to be first…"

The officer, who was white, took another step back. As he lowered the light, his eyes were all over me, trying to size up the situation. I regained my composure but my heart rate was still double what it was two minutes ago.

He took a third step back and said, "Okay…okay…," lowering his light to the ground. The officer looked a little confused. He stared at me for another second, then sighed in resignation and flicked off his light. I saw him raise his hands as if to say, *I give up*. Then the officer shook his head, turned on his heel, and walked down the sidewalk, muttering to himself.

Did he believe me? Did the officer think I was drunk—or more trouble sober? Did he let me off the hook because I was white? The questions swirled through my mind as I sat back down on the sidewalk. "Welcome to Seattle," I said to no one as I threw the blanket back over my shoulders and leaned against the union hall door again.

Silence once more enveloped me. Shaking my head and looking down, I said, "So this is what it's come to…the college honor student sleeping on the sidewalk, harassed by the police while trying—and so far failing—to get a job." I'd been at it for a month now: going through the want ads, following up on job openings, tracking down leads, hustling every opportunity, and coming up empty handed. I became desperate, and in the process was disgusted with my situation and with myself. I stared blankly into the darkness. "If my classmates from college could see me now…" My humiliation was complete, and I had started off so well, begun on such an optimistic note, just a month ago.

Back in June, I had relocated to Seattle with my bachelor's degree in hand, landing at my older sister's house. Nancy lived with her husband in the southeast part of the city, in an aging bungalow in the Beacon Hill neighborhood. With two small kids, their tiny house was already crowded, so I slept on the worn green couch in their living room.

"Hey, little brother," Nancy had greeted me at the door, wrapping me in a warm bear hug, her fingers pressing into my arms. "Welcome to Seattle. This is going to be *great*. I've got everything fixed up for you." Always the big sister, Nancy probably had a toothbrush set aside for me in the bathroom.

That first afternoon I sat, coffee cup in hand, poring over the newspaper in Nancy's kitchen. It was the late 1970s, disco music was sweeping the country, and finding a job began with scouring the Help Wanted section of the *Seattle Times*. The page was large, and the newsprint was small, so by my rose-colored calculation, there were hundreds, maybe even thousands, of job openings waiting to be filled.

Reality hit hard the following morning when I tried to track down addresses in the city and follow up on applications. I wasn't familiar with Seattle, didn't know the layout of the downtown streets, couldn't even find parking. When I finally made a connection, all I did was fill out paperwork and receive a polite "Thanks, we'll let you know." By the end of the first day, I'd turned in a total of four applications.

Days wore on and I continued filling out applications, but I didn't have any follow-up meetings or interviews. I heard the same "Thanks, we'll be in touch if we need you," but no one got in touch. No one needed me.

In my own naive way, I'd assumed that if I went to college, worked hard, and earned a degree, a well-paying job would automatically fall into my lap. As a white, entitled college-educated male, it was a foregone conclusion that I would end up with a great-paying job. I expected some older, white, entitled college-educated male to hand it to me. In retrospect, that was so presumptuous. I didn't consider the things that needed to happen between earning my degree and being offered a job. So…applications continued going out blindly, without anything coming back.

I spent four weeks getting nowhere, and I tried to keep up a brave face as misery built up inside me. My efforts in college had been rewarded with recognition, good grades, and a diploma. Now I put the same level of dedication into job hunting and totally struck out. Truth was, during the Jimmy Carter years, the economy was floundering, college degree or not.

I tried to remain hopeful when, tracking down another lead, I pulled up to the Todd Shipyard parking lot on Harbor Island. Ambling to the main gate, a uniformed security guard directed me to an aging wooden building that needed new paint. I found the personnel office on the ground floor, walked in, and asked if they were hiring. The man behind the desk stopped what he was doing, leaned back in his creaking metal chair, and set his glasses on the desk. "Yes," he said slowly, "we have openings. What craft are you?"

What craft am I? All I could think of was arts and crafts, like in elementary school, but my unsuccessful job hunting had taught me not to verbalize off the top of my head. Playing it safe, I didn't say anything. My blank look was enough to tell him I needed information.

"Craft is another word for trade." He paused and then explained, "A trade is like welder or pipe fitter, or shipwright or rigger. Those are all shipbuilding trades."

I might not have found a job yet, but I'd developed enough sense by now to leave "I was a biology major" and "I graduated with honors" and other such statements out of the conversation. "Oh…ah…I'm not any of those."

"Well then, if you don't have a specific craft, you'll want to hire on as a laborer."

Laborer? My thoughts stuttered. I'm going to hire on as a *laborer?* But I was a biology major…I graduated with honors.

I had to make a decision. Did I want to be a laborer? No, but I did need a job. Any job. *Come on,* I reminded myself, *this really isn't a tough call.* I'd heard nothing back from the stack of applications I'd turned in all over town. I needed to move off my sister's couch. I wanted the money because I was going broke. On top of that, I was slowly cracking up. All of a sudden, *laborer* started sounding pretty appealing. *I needed the goddamn paycheck.*

Staring at me, he patiently asked, "So do you want to hire on as a laborer?"

Laborer. Right. *Just go for it.* "Sure," I said, nodding. "Do you have an application I can fill out?"

"No, it doesn't work that way. All of our tradespeople come to us through union halls. You see, each craft—each trade—is represented by a specific union. You go and join a union, and when we have a need for someone in a particular craft, say a boilermaker, we call the Boilermaker's Union and they send someone to us. Anyway"—he looked down and rummaged around in his desk drawer—"if you don't already have a specific craft, you'll want to join the laborers union. Here." He handed me a card. "Go sign up with these guys. They'll get you started."

The card read "Ship Scalers, Dry Dock, and Boat Yard Workers Union" along with a street address in the Central District. My eyes lit up as a genuine smile of relief relaxed my face. I felt lighter. I might have even heard music playing. "Thanks," I said.

It only took me four weeks, but I finally had a solid lead on a job.

CHAPTER 3

The next day I stood at the corner of 23rd Street and East Madison, placing me at the north end of the Central District, home to Seattle's African American community. The Central District enjoyed a rich cultural and musical heritage, counting itself as home to Quincy Jones and Jimi Hendrix. A teenage Ray Charles launched his career here, as did Sir Mix-a-Lot, DJing parties at the local Boys and Girls Clubs.

In the late 1970s, the neighborhood was about seventy percent Black and had been the epicenter of the civil rights movement for the people of Seattle.

This was a fitting location for the Ship Scalers Union Hall, because its membership was heavily African American. It hadn't always been so. The union started out downtown, in the Belltown area, originally composed of Western European shipyard workers, mostly Norwegians from Seattle's Ballard neighborhood. Prior to the Second World War, unions actively discriminated against Black people, barring them from membership or, in some cases, segregating minority shipyard workers into "auxiliary locals" of a union. As Blacks were integrated into the US Army, progress slowly crept forward for minority workers in the shipyards.

Change was snail-like across the economic landscape and especially along the waterfront, but a door eventually creaked opened for Black workers in the shipyards. It wasn't much of an opening, though. The craft unions, representing skilled workers, continued to discriminate by and large, but the Ship Scalers Union—the laborers' union—opened membership to minority workers. Ship scaling was the least desirable work in the shipyard: dirty and dangerous, not to mention the lowest paid. But this was the only door open to African Americans, so Blacks walked through it. African Americans became the majority in the Ship Scalers Union, eventually making up about ninety percent of its membership in the years after the war. The Ship Scalers went on to become a progressive voice in Seattle for social change, integration issues, and civil rights.

Standing in front of the union hall that morning, I studied the peeling paint. With "Ship Scalers Union Local 541" posted over the door, the building's rundown appearance belied its venerable history of activism and fighting for social justice. That Thursday the hall just looked tired and worn out.

Walking inside, I immediately felt out of place. Earlier I'd scouted two corporate job openings downtown—so, dressed for success—I wore a suit and tie. Against one wall was a row of rickety wooden chairs and four Black men talking. They all wore faded gray coveralls and scuffed black work boots. The men looked up for a second, said nothing to me, then went back to talking among themselves.

I don't belong here. All of a sudden, I sensed how white I was, and I wondered for a second, *Is this how it feels?*

I'd known two or three Black students at college—there were no Black kids at my high school—so, *was this the sort of feeling they experienced each day in college?* Was this what they felt, magnified on a much greater scale, every time they walked into a classroom full of white people?

I walked past the men to the opposite side of the room, next to an office front with what looked like a plexiglass bank teller's window, the kind with a semicircular opening. A thin, ancient Black man leaned back in an old swivel chair in the office. Approaching the window, I bent forward and said, "I'd like to join the Ship Scalers Union."

The man didn't look up. He didn't even move. Instead, he took a long breath, then exhaled "Eight a.m. call" in a voice charred by cigarettes.

I ducked down a little, bringing my face closer to the semicircular opening. "That's when I can sign up?"

He still didn't look up, but the lines in his face deepened as he repeated, "Eight a.m. call," then swiveled in his chair, turning away from me.

Do I wait here? Do I say something?

I stood there, head down, feeling the men's eyes from across the room on my back, and realized nothing else was going to happen. I put my hands in my pockets and quietly left, driving back to my sister's place. Stopping along the way at the giant Sears store on Third Avenue South, I bought coveralls and black, midcalf-high, steel-toed work boots.

Friday morning I was up early, parking down the street from the hall. It was a quarter to eight, and I walked down the sidewalk, counting eight or nine people—mostly men and all older than me—lined up by the door, some stomping their feet to stay warm. *Just in time for the 8 a.m. call.* Walking to the back, wearing my brand-new coveralls, I was met with eyes neither welcoming nor disapproving. I was the only white guy.

Alone at the end of the line, I kept checking my watch: ten till eight... five till eight...then, right on the money, the door to the union hall swung open. The line quietly filed in as people queued up in front of the plexiglass teller's window, and a deep, now familiar gravelly voice barked out, "Call for four at Lockheed, ship repair, days." One at a time, the first four people bent down to the window and gave their names. The thin man wrote down each one, and after the four left, the rest of the line queued up expectantly.

"Call for two at Todd, ship repair, swing." The next two people gave their names, and then the man in the office placed a semicircular piece of plexiglass, cut to fit, into the window, sealing it up. He turned around with the list of names, sat down at his desk, and picked up the phone.

Was that it?

"Show's over," the person in front of me said as people turned to leave. I hesitated for a second, looked around, then followed everyone out. The show *was* over. This was going to be a little harder than I thought. Obviously, I had to be there earlier for the Monday-morning call.

The weekend came and went. With Nancy's living-room couch serving as my bedroom for the last month, my sister's small home became even smaller. She'd made a nice enough space for me, with sheets and a pillow and blanket on the couch, like my own miniature bed, but it was still my sister's living-room sofa. Nancy was going to great lengths to make me feel at home, but I needed to get out of there and get a place of my own.

Monday morning, I pulled up in front of the union hall a little after seven, this time counting five people in line. *Okay...makes me number six.* Standing in line, I made some small talk with two guys in front of me. With an hour to kill, I learned (a) the man behind the plexiglass was J.J. Williams, president of the Ship Scalers Union; (b) most people were sent to either Todd Shipyard or Lockheed Shipyard; (c) calls were for day shift, swing shift, or graveyard; and (d) people were sent to either "ship repair" or "new construction."

I absorbed the information, although I didn't fully appreciate all the implications yet. Precisely at eight o'clock the union hall door opened, and we filed in. By now there were ten or twelve people in line and I smiled, feeling confident being number six. From behind the window J.J.'s voice rang out, "Call for three at Lockheed, ship repair, swing." After the first three people in line gave their names and left, the plexiglass insert went back into the window. J.J. sat down to phone in the names. End of story.

This is getting frustrating.

I had the rest of the day to kill and no job openings to pursue. At least I knew the routine at the union hall now. *Tomorrow morning I'm going to be first in line.* I didn't feel like returning to Nancy's living-room couch to sleep that night, so after changing, I left my sister a note on the couch, then drove around the city. Ending up in Chinatown, I bought a bowl of noodles at a little restaurant. I ate slowly, drank a lot of tea, and wasted enough time to arrive at the union hall around midnight. That's when I had my encounter with the Seattle Police officer, who was the last person I saw until about six, when two guys walked by, one white and one Black, both a little younger than me.

"You waitin' for the eight a.m. call?" they asked. I nodded. "Mind if we join you?"

Their names were Willy and Derek, buddies who graduated from Garfield High School that spring. They heard ship scaling was a good-paying gig and were impressed when I told them I'd arrived at midnight to be the first person in line.

Time passed quickly as we fell into conversation, and by eight o'clock there were six people in line behind us. The door swung open right on time, and I marched into the union hall with a self-satisfied grin. *First in line!*

The union president, J.J., looked up from his chair and barked, "No calls today!"

We stood there, momentarily frozen, as J.J.'s words bounced off us. *Christ! What's it gonna take?* I rolled my eyes and turned away. *So much for being first in line.*

Looking at Willy and Derek, I cleared my throat and swallowed my frustration. "Guess that means I'll see you guys tomorrow morning."

"Yeah, *early* in the morning," Willy shot back, a little bleary eyed.

I arrived at midnight, and my new friends showed up a little after one. This time hanging out in front of the union hall was fun: with Willy and Derek, it was like a junior high sleepover. I had my blanket, Willy brought two sleeping bags, and Derek showed up with a bag of Doritos and a box of Twinkies, which we devoured. We talked the whole evening, and among other things, they told me about a couple people who were shot one night down the street from us at the Honeysuckle Tavern. *Glad there's three of us here tonight*, I thought.

By eight o'clock a dozen people were in line, and bang on the dot, the union hall door swung open. Once again, I led the procession to the teller's window. This time, J.J. said the magic words. "Call for two at Lockheed, ship repair, days."

Finally! Being first in line, I couldn't wait to give my name, but I wavered. I knew Willy and Derek hoped to be called out together, and this was a call for two. I backed away...after all, they *had* brought the food last night. "You guys go ahead of me. It's a call for two." Willy and Derek went around me and gave their names while I prayed that J.J. would keep talking.

My anxiety was short-lived. "Call for four, Todd, ship repair, swing."

This time it was my name J.J. was writing down. "So I just show up at Todd Shipyard?" I asked.

"Right," J.J. replied. "I'll phone your name over there, so be at the yard by four o'clock today. They'll be expecting you."

"Okay." I nodded. "Thanks." I shook hands with Willy and Derek, wishing them luck, then bolted from the hall. Just like that, I had a job. I possessed identity. I had ceased to be Mike Nolan College Student, and was no longer Mike Nolan Unemployed. *I was Mike Nolan Ship Scaler*, and I couldn't wait to tell somebody—my folks back home, my sister Nancy—anybody. I had no idea what a ship scaler did, but that didn't matter. At four o'clock I'd find out.

CHAPTER 4

At a quarter to four in the afternoon, I pulled up to a crowded Todd Shipyard parking lot, anxious to become a ship scaler and earn a paycheck. The early fall weather wasn't promising: ashen skies, mild temperatures; but I optimistically considered it a light gray canvas on which to paint my first day.

When I told the sleepy, white-haired security guard at the main gate I was sent from the union hall, he pointed to a rack of different-colored hard hats. "Put one of those on." I grabbed the hat closest to me, which was white, but when I turned back to him, he shook his head. "No…no…not that one. Put that back. What craft are you?"

"Ship scaler?"

"Then grab one of those orange hard hats." He handed me a blank manila-colored punch card. "Here, print your name at the top—and print it so they can read it, or you won't get paid." He pointed to a small clock mounted on a post at the end of a huge metal rack full of timecards. "Punch it there." I stuck one end of my timecard into a slot beneath the clock and—*stamp!*—the time appeared on my card. "Now take it over there." He pointed in the direction of the company offices.

By now the other three scalers from the union hall had shown up. While the guard got them going, I walked to the administration building. The man sitting in the personnel office was the same person who had directed me to the Ship Scalers Union. He was dressed in white coveralls and a white hard hat. I could tell he recognized me when I walked in, but he didn't acknowledge me. This time, I sensed more than physical distance between us across his desk.

A minute later the other scalers came in and stood beside me. The personnel manager said, "Okay…you four will be working on the *Thomaston*. She's tied up to the pier across from the shipways. This is Henderson." He gestured to another man who had silently walked into the office behind us. He was a short, solid, powerfully built Black man with a thick mustache. I could tell from his demeanor that he was not a new recruit. "Henderson is your leadman. He'll show you what to do."

Henderson wore dirty blue coveralls. A laminated Todd Shipyard badge showing a headshot and barcode was clipped to his breast pocket. His hard hat was orange like ours, but it had a large capital "L" on the front. His commanding presence exuded unspoken confidence; in other words, he was everything I was not.

"Why don't you gimme your timecards," Henderson said in a low monotone. Collecting the cards, he slowly read each name, then tucked the stack into his shirt pocket. "Okay…follow me."

The four of us shuffled out behind Henderson and followed him to the tool room—a misnomer, because it was a cavernous tool *warehouse*. Long aisles of metal shelves were piled high with boxes and crates, and a forklift moved back and forth in the recesses of the space. We lined up along the front, leaning on the dull silver sheet-metal counter.

"Canvas work gloves," Henderson said to one of the men behind the counter. He took Henderson's badge and scanned the barcode. We were issued safety glasses, and Henderson pointed to a box of earplug packets on the counter. "Grab y'all some of those."

After that, he looked at us with absolutely no expression and said, "Okay," which I guess was his way of saying, "Follow me, guys, and I'll take you to the worksite."

We walked past a massive Navy vessel on the shipway, a "fast frigate." Two towering cranes wheeled up and down the pier alongside it, loading pallets onto the vessel's main deck. Scaffolding had been erected all along the hull, with three or four guys perched in various places, welding. Golden sparks flowed down the sleek gray hull in narrow, shimmering waterfalls.

Throughout the yard, workers moved in every direction—carrying tools, dragging hoses, lugging equipment—with forklifts driving in between them all. I paused for a second and looked around, pressed in by the noise and frenzied activity all around me. Everything was in motion. It was loud and hurried and seemed erratic, but at the same time the movement possessed an energetic rhythm and geometry: *perfectly organized chaos*. I loved being in the center of it all.

Past the shipways, Henderson led us down a long wooden pier with two vessels tied up to it. On the far side, I recognized the familiar green and white markings of a Washington State ferry, and on the close side was the *Thomaston*, a haze-gray Navy vessel with an enormous "28" painted on her bow.

"Is this the boat we're working on?" I asked Henderson, walking down the pier.

"Ship," he corrected, without breaking stride.

The four of us followed Henderson up a lengthy aluminum gangway, climbing from the pier to the main deck of the *Thomaston*. One of the scalers behind me, who obviously had more experience, leaned forward. "You can put a boat on a ship, but you can't put a ship on a boat."

I turned around. "Okay, I get it. It has to do with size."

"Uh-huh."

"One's a lot bigger than the other. Like 'life *boat*' versus 'battle *ship*.'"

"You're learnin'" was the laconic reply.

One of the first things I had to figure out was the language of the shipyard. We didn't walk "downstairs" or "past a window"; we went "below decks," "down a ladder," "past a porthole." I knew port from starboard, but those terms didn't flow naturally from me yet. Every time I used the word *starboard*, I flexed my right hand. *Starboard* had more letters than *port*, so it was right as opposed to left, since *right* had more letters than *left*. Not exactly sophisticated seamanship.

Henderson led us below decks and through what seemed like a maze, until we came to a compartment—not a *room*. "This is where day shift left off."

The compartment was empty except for four aluminum ladders and a big bale of rags. Heavy brown paper covered the floor—the *deck*—and the light fixtures were wrapped in clear plastic sheeting and masking tape.

"Y'all get ya a ladder." Henderson bent down with a pair of pliers and clipped the baling wire on the bundle of rags. "We're gonna get this space ready to paint."

"We're going to paint it?" I asked.

"Fuck no. We're gonna get this fucker *ready* to be painted," he said matter-of-factly. "The fucking painters gonna fucking paint it."

The look on my face was probably something like, "*there's a lot they don't teach you in college*," but I managed to smile, realizing I'd finally heard Henderson utter more than three words in a row. I was catching on to something else about shipyard terminology—something that would become abundantly clear in the next few days: everyone used the word *fuck*, or some permutation of it, continually. With a little bit of imagination, people used the word as a verb, a noun, an adjective, and an adverb. And it went on like that, *all the fucking time.*

"Get y'all some rags too," Henderson said, "and wipe down the fucking overhead."

"Right." The other guys grabbed handfuls of rags and started up the ladders. The overhead—the ceiling in the compartment—was exposed steel I-beams. They were dusty, and here and there I found stubby, burned ends of spent welding rods. My first eight hours as a ship scaler consisted of wiping down I-beams.

My second and third nights at Todd were just like the first: Henderson would take us to a compartment—"*a fucking compartment*" —a little farther down the passageway from the night before, where I could see that the painters on day shift had painted the compartments we'd already cleaned. I wiped I-beams every night for eight hours, the job lasted three days, and at the end of my third shift, Henderson caught up with me.

"Here." He handed me a slip of pink paper.

"What's this?"

"It's what it fucking says it is." He pointed to the bold lettering at the top of the pink carbon copy: Reduction in Force.

In my head, I was asking myself how I could be so smart—I had graduated *cum laude*—and at the same time be so ignorant. My eyebrows went up as I stammered, "So this is…?"

"You got an R-I-F, man—you know—you got '*riffed*.'" Henderson shrugged. "This here's your fucking *pink slip*. You been laid off."

Right, I thought, *there is a lot they don't teach you in college, but I'm learnin'.*

The next morning I was back in line, picturing the plexiglass semicircle and anticipating J.J.'s charcoal voice. This time I didn't line up at midnight; I knew the first few people would show up between six and seven, so that's when I got there. As it turned out, I was third in line, which was perfect. J.J.'s first call was "Four at Lockheed, ship repair, days."

The four of us—different people from those I'd worked with before—met at Lockheed's Yard Two, situated in West Seattle, across the Duwamish Waterway from Yard One. The work routine at Lockheed was the same as at Todd. Ship scalers wore orange hard hats, and other crafts were color coded as well: blue for welders, black for machinists, yellow for electricians, and so on. The one hard hat you paid attention to was white. Union workers wore colored hats, while company employees wore white hats and white coveralls—symbolizing they were in charge. We referred to these individuals as "white hats," which made me think of television Westerns I watched as a kid, where the "good guys" wore white hats. I didn't know if these people were good or not, but I picked up on the "good guys against the bad guys" motif, or maybe it was simply "us against them."

As a union member, I was connected to guys in other crafts, but I sensed a gulf, a wide divide, between union workers and white hats. You made sure to stay busy if one of them was around; otherwise you'd catch hell, earning yourself a good ass-chewing from your leadman. The advice other scalers gave me was to "keep moving, be working, don't stop. And never, ever stand around with your hands in your pockets."

At Lockheed we were issued safety glasses and earplugs from the tool room, just like at Todd. The safety glasses were thick and nerdy looking, like the ones worn in junior high wood shop, with heavy plastic lenses and dark horn-rimmed frames. They looked like they could stop a bullet. But in the shipyard, where there was so much obvious potential for an eye injury, it didn't bother me to be wearing stupid-looking glasses—the thicker, the better. Also, since I sometimes ended up working in painfully loud spaces, like the boiler room or the engine room, my earplugs went in the moment I entered the shipyard and stayed in until quitting time.

The workers at Lockheed were organized the same way as at Todd, with four or five scalers working together as a crew at a specific site on the ship. Each crew was supervised by someone with an "L" on their hard hat, like Henderson. The leadman reported to the craft foreman, who wore a capital "F" on their hard hat. The foreman answered to a white hat, the "company man" higher up the ladder. Supervising all of the white-hats was the production manager, sitting on top of the pyramid. As a lowly new-hire ship scaler it would be weeks before I met anyone higher up than my leadman.

That first day at Lockheed, our leadman took the four of us to an exterior passageway on the main deck of a gigantic Naval ship, to an area that had been sandblasted. The space was dirty and at the same time clean. The newly-blasted steel bulkhead shone a dull silver, but an inch or two of gritty black sand covered the deck, residue from the sandblasting.

Our job was to remove all sand from the bulkhead, the overhead beams, and then the deck, but first we had to rip down the heavy green canvas that had been wrapped and duct-taped over the fixtures to protect them during blasting. The canvas covered lights, switches, vent openings, and miles of cable and wiring. Each time I tore down some canvas, a small black-particle cloud of sand came down with it. I dodged as best I could, but it would fall down my shirt and down my back; eventually it got into my mouth and I was able to taste it. When I spat gobs of black sand onto the deck, our leadman gave us each a white paper mask to wear. By the end of the shift, my mask was black.

Once we had torn down all the protective canvas and stuffed it into garbage bags, a couple of us got up on ladders and started blowing down the overhead with high-pressure air hoses, clearing out the remaining sand from the steel beams and the nooks and crannies around the ducts and hoses and wiring. The other scalers on the crew cleaned up behind us, using brooms, foxtails, and dustpans. When the space was totally sand free, it was ready for the painters.

As the shift wore on, it took just a couple hours for the repetitious work to become numbingly mindless. Still, my surroundings were totally different from those of any work I'd done before, and I would catch myself wondering, *How'd I end up here?*

You needed a paycheck, I told myself. *That's how.*

The four of us cleaned overheads for two days, then I got laid off again.

The next call I got was for three scalers to ship repair at Todd for the graveyard shift, which began at midnight. I was excited about getting a graveyard call, because it meant a ten percent "shift differential" or increase in my paycheck. If I could work for a month or so on graveyard, I'd have enough money set aside for rent. I could finally get my own apartment!

The routine for graveyard was similar to day shift and swing, just quieter, because there were fewer people working in the shipyard at night. The only difference in getting started was when the graveyard leadman took the three of us to the tool room and we were each issued rain gear and a straight scraping hoe to go with the usual safety equipment. The bright yellow plastic jacket and pants didn't make sense to me, since it was a perfectly clear, cloudless night. If I had questions, though, I'd learned to keep them to myself. *Don't worry*, I thought, *they'll tell you soon enough. And if they don't, you'll figure it out on your own.*

I tucked my rain gear under one arm as we followed the leadman to the dry dock and down underneath a 200-foot-long barge elevated on stacks of wooden blocks thicker than railroad ties. Out of the water, the vessel looked three times larger, like a beached whale. Walking under the imposing, oversized hull gave me a weird feeling. *If a big wave hit the dock, this monster would tumble down and crush us.* No one else seemed to care, though, and I guessed that the blocks and timbers supporting the hull looked sturdy enough.

The barge was blocked up five feet above the dry dock deck. Those of us who were over five feet tall could walk around underneath it by ducking a little as we stepped over hoses and electrical cords running everywhere. A number of floodlights lit up the area beneath the barge as bright as day, which felt surreal surrounded by pitch black outside. Looking up at the surface of the hull, I saw decaying sea life that had grown around brown, rusty patches. Barnacles, plume worms, and seaweed—dying and rotting—still clung tenaciously to the metal hull. That rank smell hit hard.

"Get your gear on," our leadman said, and we all struggled into our yellow rain clothes. At first, I was surprised to see the other two scalers pull their hoods up over their heads and put their hard hats on over that, but it would all make sense to me in a few minutes.

We grabbed our scraping hoes as the leadman pointed to the underside of the barge. "Start here and work your way aft." Then he walked away to have a smoke.

"I'll start here, Nolan," the guy next to me said. "Why don't you start right over there?" He pointed to a spot ten feet away, then raised his hoe and started scraping. I did the same and, for the next four hours, I completed some of the dirtiest, smelliest work of my life, scraping rust and dead marine life overhead with an iron hoe. Globs of the gunk plopped on top of me, splattering my safety glasses and falling down the back of my collar. It only took a minute before I stopped and pulled my rain hood up, as the other guys had done, cinching it tight around my face.

At 4:00 in the morning, we broke for lunch, but I'd lost my appetite. Instead, I slept on one of the wooden benches in the locker room. When the other scalers woke me for the second half of the shift, I had reservations about returning—but I still wanted that shift differential. If I could stay on graveyard, even for a week, I'd collect a fat paycheck on Friday. So I stuck with it, enduring four more hours of scraping—and dodging—dead sea life.

At the end of the shift, we were all laid off. So much for the fat Friday paycheck.

I collapsed on a bench in the locker room, a stinking mess. *One miserable shift on graveyard, followed by a pink slip.* Discouraged, exhausted, and dirty, I felt as if my arms were going to fall off. As I lay back on the bench and tried to stretch out my hunched spine, the comment "you're learnin'" echoed in my mind.

I heard the 8:00 a.m. whistle blow, meaning I couldn't get back to the union hall in time for the next call. "I don't care," I said to no one. "I need a shower, some breakfast, and I need to sleep. Preferably in that order."

CHAPTER 5

Work continued on in the same vein: I'd be sent from the union hall to jobs in ship repair at Lockheed and Todd, only to receive a pink slip two or three days later and be out of work for a couple days. About eight hundred people belonged to the Ship Scalers Union, and ninety percent of them were working. With robust shipbuilding activity at both yards, people constantly came and went from the union hall. Without steady work, though, I kept feeling like an outsider looking in, always the new guy, but at least I was learning the tricks of the ship scaler trade as I went along.

Itching to vacate Nancy's couch, I started looking for a place to live, checking out apartments on Capitol Hill and putting rent money aside. To save up first and last month's rent, the challenge was to get more than two or three days of work in a row, especially in the event that an apartment manager phoned one of the shipyards to verify my employment on one of my "laid off" days.

This particular morning, I was part of a day-shift call for three at Todd, working alongside Nguyen, a slight, male Vietnamese scaler, and Mavis, a Black woman in her sixties. Very few women worked in the shipyard, but the ones who did were almost all scalers. Apparently, the Ship Scalers Union opened the doors to waterfront work not only for African American males but for women, too.

Mavis, Nguyen, and I were getting outfitted in the tool room when Nguyen lit a cigarette and offered me one. I hadn't smoked as a kid, unless you counted the occasional Camel I snuck from my dad's pack when he wasn't looking, but once I joined the work force in the shipyard, it seemed as though everyone smoked. I'd be working with a crew, we'd take a break, and everybody would light up. So I started smoking to fit in, as part of the job. It must have been part of the job, because I never smoked outside of work.

We three were assigned to a job in the engine room of a freighter, mucking out "bilges," the interior, curved sections of the hull in the very bottom of the ship. The tool room issued a stack of plastic garbage bags, along with rubber boots and elbow-length rubber gloves. Good thing, because this particular job turned out to be even more disgusting than scraping dead barnacles underneath a barge.

Today's job put Mavis, Nguyen, and me in close contact, giving us the opportunity to talk, and I asked them about being sent from the union hall. Mavis's experiences were similar to mine, but she had been with the union a little longer and knew more about how it all worked.

"First, there's the difference between ship repair and new construction," Mavis told me. "You see, it takes a couple *years* to build a full-size Navy ship. You go from one piece of steel"—Mavis held up one hand, making a space between her thumb and index finger—"that's the keel." Then, stretching out both hands wide, she smiled. "And you go all the way to the ship being built and launched. So if you're on a crew in *new* construction, you're gonna stick around for a while."

"Especially if you get the call early on," Nguyen added, in lightly accented English.

"Ship repair jobs," Mavis said, "never last more than a couple days. A ship comes in for repair when something is broke, so it can't do what a ship does." She shook her head. "The ship owner is losing money every hour the ship is sitting in repair. So, the work of fixin' whatever is broke gets done quick, with all three shifts running 'round the clock, twenty-four seven. As soon as possible, the ship goes back in the water, back to making money for the owner. That means ship repair jobs are always short-term."

"And our work, what scalers do," Nguyen said, "like cleaning or sandblasting…a lot of it happens during a repair."

"Sometimes only during repair," Mavis said with a knowing smile. "A ship would never be dry docked just to be scraped or sandblasted. Too expensive. It's here to be fixed."

"And once that's done, we all get laid off," Nguyen added.

"Okay…so how do I get a call for new construction?"

"I guess you gotta be standing there in the union hall when they just gonna start building." Mavis laughed. "Fact is, most days the calls outta the hall are for repair."

"We have to go wherever J.J. sends us," Nguyen said, "unless you got seniority."

"Yeah, good ol' sen-i-or-i-ty," Mavis sang, stretching out the word. "That's what we all want. The way the union is organized, you have to work ten consecutive days to get your seniority and become a registered member of the Ship Scalers Union."

Ten days didn't sound like much, but by now I knew that working ten straight days at the same location was a lot more challenging than it sounded. I hadn't gotten half of that. All my work had been in ship repair, with most jobs lasting two or three days.

"Your tenth day becomes your seniority date," Mavis said. "That's when you officially join the union."

"And according to union rules," Nguyen said, "when a layoff comes, scalers are let go in order of seniority…least senior laid off first, most senior last."

"Everybody memorizes their seniority date." Mavis smiled.

Of course they did. It was our one measure of job security, part of our union protection, and it was the only way I'd ever get empowered in this setting.

Hearing the leadman walk by on an overhead platform, we got to work. The engine room had several levels, the bilges being in the very bottom of the space. Any liquids spilled on an upper level eventually drained down here.

"Have you ever cleaned bilges?" Nguyen grinned.

"Why do you ask?"

"Because they're *gross,*" Mavis said.

"I've seen machinists and boilermakers pitch cigarette butts and candy wrappers and trash into the bilges," Nguyen added, "so we gonna clean the engine room's *garbage can* today."

"People spit into them," Mavis said, then added in a lower voice, "and some men do worse than that."

Nguyen shook his head in disgust. "The Sani-Cans are up on the main deck, so some of the men don't bother making the trip. They 'go' in the bilges."

I groaned and rolled my eyes. "And that's what we're cleaning?"

"Come on, Nolan," Mavis said, "You got gloves, don't you?"

"And we got this." Nguyen defiantly held up a dustpan, like a weapon. "Prepare for battle, *bilge rat*."

Pulling my rubber gloves practically up to my chin, I knelt by the bilges. I dug my gloved hands in, straightening my back to keep my face as far from the moldering slime as possible. Mavis held open a plastic bag while I scooped up handfuls of muck, and Nguyen used his dustpan like a shovel. Once a bag contained a few gallons of the vile sludge, Nguyen tied it off, and we took turns slinging them over a shoulder and hauling them up to the main deck. From there, we lugged the bags down the gangway and out to the pier, where we tossed them into a dumpster.

It was a filthy, stinking job—one that made me want to stand in the middle of the engine room and scream, *"I just want everyone to know I graduated cum laude at Gonzaga University!"*

Mavis noticed my sardonic grin and must have read my mind. "Hey, we're scalers," she said, " an' you know that means we *always* get the dirtiest work."

The bilge cleaning lasted for two days, and on the third day, Mavis, Nguyen, and I were assigned to general clean-up around the ship: picking up trash, coiling hoses, sweeping decks. "This sort of cleaning means one thing," Mavis warned as we began our work. At the end of the shift, I found out she was right: the three of us were laid off.

When I got back to Nancy's house that evening, I tossed my pink slip on the kitchen counter.

"Another layoff, huh?" Nancy asked, wrinkling her brow.

"Yeah, and I'm beginning to wonder...should I keep doing this?" I leaned against the counter and folded my arms across my chest. "This isn't working. If I can't get on full time, I'll never get ahead. I can't, you know, get to the next step, get a place of my own." In my mind, I could see the same pattern going on forever. It wasn't as if *trying harder* was going to keep me from getting laid off over and over again. *What was that definition of insanity? Repeating the same thing and expecting different results?*

Nancy clearly sensed my frustration because she wrapped an arm around my shoulder and gave me a hug. "You're welcome to stay here as long as you like. You know that."

"I know...you're great for giving me a place to stay. Really." Now I was hugging her. "You're the best big sister. I appreciate you looking out for me, but I can't make things happen working two or three days a week. I gotta somehow take that next step so I can get out on my own, so I can make it." I *did* appreciate Nancy and everything she was doing for me, but in some weird, guilty way I also felt that by continuing to lean on my sister, I wasn't fighting hard enough to break into the next level.

The following morning, I was back at the union hall, and J.J.'s call returned me to Lockheed Yard One, on a crew with three other guys assigned to scrape the underside of a barge. As we approached the dry dock, I could see the barge was blocked up about four feet high.

"Are they going to raise that thing?" I asked one of the scalers.

He started laughing.

"That's why we got these," another scaler said, holding up a specialized pair of shoes the tool room had issued us along with our rain gear and scraping hoe. The shoes he tossed me were short, thick flip-flops with straps. Watching the other guys, I copied what they were doing and buckled them over my kneecaps.

We proceeded to scrape the entire length of the barge, two hundred feet down and two hundred feet back, with four feet of clearance, crawling on our knees. The shift was interminable, and as time dragged along, my knees got sore, then began to throb, then went numb and turned to jelly. When the whistle blew and we broke for lunch, I leaned on my hoe with both hands and climbed it to stand, straightening my back and wobbling on unsteady legs.

The second half of the shift was equally painful and never-ending. By now I was bringing my own smokes to work, and to break the monotony and keep myself going during the second shift, I chain-smoked a pack of Camels. My body was on autopilot and my mind occupied a nicotine-fueled zone where there was no *thinking*, only *scraping*.

On one level, I could console myself by knowing I was performing real "ship scaler" work: scaling the surface of a ship, just as you'd scale the side of a fish before cooking it. By definition, ship scalers chipped, scraped, scoured, and blasted the exterior and interior of ships to remove dirt, sea life, old paint, rust, and anything else deemed undesirable for a vessel's surface. For some jobs, we used small hand-held tools like paint scrapers or wire brushes; other jobs required larger tools like two-handed pneumatic disc grinders or a needle gun—a pipe-shaped pneumatic tool with vibrating steel rods sticking out one end. But these implements of destruction were minor league compared to the tools of the trade at the top of the ship scaling pyramid: the sandblaster's hood and high-pressure hose.

Sandblasters made up a small subset of workers within the Ship Scalers Union, a brotherhood a cut above the rest, at least in my mind. I hadn't met any sandblasters yet, but I saw these guys at both Todd and Lockheed. You couldn't miss them. In addition to wearing full rain gear—whatever the weather—over their coveralls, sandblasters sported thick black hoods covering their heads, shoulders, and midsections. The hoods each had a rectangular two-by-four-inch plate of safety glass in the front, like a scuba mask. And like a diver, sandblasters breathed through an air hose that ran under the hood.

Due to the specialized work they performed, sandblasters didn't get laid off. The shipyard could afford to have laborers—bilge muckers like me—

come and go, but sandblasters had expertise—they were skilled craftsmen—so the shipyard had a vested interest in retaining them. I didn't know how to become a sandblaster; I wasn't aware of the training involved, but I knew I wanted to be one. I considered it far more appealing to be seen as a craftsman as opposed to a laborer. Plus, I was desperate to quit getting laid off.

A week later, I took a chance and signed a monthly rental agreement for an apartment on Capitol Hill, in the heart of Seattle. My longest stretch of consecutive work at this point was four days, so getting laid off and not making my rent remained a constant worry. I started collecting my RIF notices and taping them to my living-room wall, slowly turning one section of my apartment pink. Then, a few weeks later, a situation presented itself during a ship repair job on a Washington State ferry. All of a sudden, I had a chance to take a shot. Totally out of character, I went out on a limb and grabbed this particular opportunity with both hands.

The union hall had sent me and two other guys to clean up around the ferry's engine room following some maintenance work. We were told to tear up and haul out all the heavy protective deck paper that had been laid down in the passageways. Papering the passageways to keep the decks clean was always the first task to be completed when a ship came in for repair work, and tearing it out was the last task once repairs were finished. Clearly, the ferry was being readied to go back into service, so the job I was on would not continue. I could see it coming: we would all be laid off at the end of the shift.

The three of us were tearing up deck paper and stuffing it into garbage bags when, twenty minutes into the shift, the leadman, a guy named Jackson, stopped us. Standing in the passageway, Jackson looked at our timecards, then at us. "Any of you guys sandblasters?"

The three of us stood there, deck paper and garbage bags in hand, and glanced at one another. It was clear to me from their disinterested expressions that the other two scalers weren't sandblasters.

I turned to Jackson. "Yeah. Me. I can blast."

I was lying through my teeth, of course, but he had no way of knowing that. Jackson hesitated for a moment, pulling at his goatee and looking at me, then back at my timecard. Jackson's bullshit meter was probably working overtime, but he hesitated and said, "So...you can blast?"

"That's right," I answered, this time with a little more confidence.

I didn't look at the other scalers, because I wouldn't have been able to keep a straight face. At any second I expected one of the guys to blurt out, "*Watchoot-*

alkinbout, muthafucka? You ain't no sandblaster. Shiiit." But the other two scalers didn't say anything, so Jackson eventually said, "Okay...come with me."

I tossed my bag of deck paper on the floor and followed Jackson up to the main deck, where a heavyset white hat with a full dark beard and glasses was waiting. Jackson pulled my timecard from his pocket and handed it to the white hat, saying, "This is Nolan."

The supervisor's eyes zeroed in on me. "And you're a sandblaster?"

I was committed at this point. Getting fired right now wasn't a whole lot worse than getting laid off at the end of the shift, so *what the hell.* I looked him straight in the eye and continued lying. "Yes, I'm a sandblaster."

His features relaxed. "Great, follow me." And off we went down the gangway and across the pier.

On the dry dock sat an imposing barge mounted on blocks, high enough to walk underneath instead of crawling on knees. Four sandblasters waited by the pier. I could hear the muffled tones of their conversation as they talked beside an oversized orange tank, about fifteen feet tall and rounded at the top, with three black hoses running out of the bottom.

The white hat brought me over to the sandblasters—all Black—who immediately stopped talking and began eying me. "This is Nolan," he announced. "He's a sandblaster. Now you guys have a full crew and should be ready to go. Do you need anything else?"

No one spoke; the sandblasters just stared at me. After waiting a second, the white hat turned on his heels and walked back down the pier to the dock office.

Not many members of the Ship Scalers Union were sandblasters. Most scalers, in fact, did not want to become sandblasters. It was dangerous, difficult work, so, given a choice, most ship scalers preferred to push a broom or scrape dead barnacles or muck out stinking bilges. Consequently, the scalers who *were* sandblasters tended to know one another, being members of a small, proud, skilled fraternity within the ranks of the union.

The white hat's receding footsteps echoed on the wooden pier behind me as I nervously exchanged glances with four Black faces. I had gotten away with lying to the leadman and to the white hat because *they* weren't sandblasters, but the men in front of me knew the score. The question in their eyes seemed to be "Who the hell is this white boy?"

This was the moment of truth, and between lying and now confronting that lie, the reality of the situation reverberated through my core. *What the hell am I getting myself into?*

One of the guys looked down and crushed out his cigarette, quietly saying, "Shiiit" as he jammed his hands into his pockets and walked away. Would he call the white hat back? Would he get me fired? Two other guys silently stared at the barge, shuffling their feet. But the fourth man, the oldest of the group—sporting a gray beard—took a step toward me and broke the silence.

"He said you're a sandblaster. Is that correct?"

Suddenly I was in court, standing in front of the judge, and I had to come clean and tell the truth. "No," I stammered, "I'm not. I lied about that."

His eyes searched mine. The silence continued, and I could feel my heart hitting against my chest like a croquet mallet. Part of me wanted to look down and see if my shirt was jumping in and out to the beat, but our eyes remained locked.

I became desperate. Unable to hold back, I blurted out, "I keep getting laid off and I can't get my seniority. I lied about being a sandblaster just now so I wouldn't get another pink slip at the end of the shift. I had to say *something* to keep my job."

More silence as the older man took this in, looking beyond me, out at the barge waiting to be sandblasted. "Well…," he said noncommittally, then he laughed softly and nodded his head. "I guess I can understand that." He sucked in his breath and nodded toward the other guys as if to say, *It'll be okay*, then turned back to me. "It's Nolan, right? I'll tell you what, Nolan. We need a hose puller, and if you can do that, we got us a whole crew. Now, you do what I tell you, and after tonight you won't have to lie no more."

"You mean you're going to teach me how to be a sandblaster?"

"Somethin' like that." He turned to the other guys. "Okay, everybody, come on," he nodded. "We can make this work. *Come on, now*…let's set up and get things goin'."

The other three men shrugged, then turned toward the orange tank. The older man repeated, "Come on," patting one of the guys on the shoulder. Then the sandblasters started walking down to the barge. Richards—the name of the grey-bearded man—turned to me. "Just follow what I tell you, Nolan, and you'll be fine." He glanced down to the barge as the other men picked up their sandblasting gear. I could see smile lines starting to form around Richards' eyes. He put his broad hand on my shoulder and started to chuckle. "Old sheep know the road, Nolan. Little lammy gotta follow."

CHAPTER 6

Richards and I stood beside the towering orange sand pot, gazing at the barge. "It takes at least three men to do a sandblast job here on the dry dock," Richards explained. "One, you got the man doing the blasting, out there at the business end of the hose." He waved an arm in the general direction of the barge. "And two"—he pointed down to where the three hoses ran into the base of the tank—"you got the man on *this here* end of the hose." Smiling and leaning back, he jerked a thumb to his chest. "And that man would be me. I'm the pot tender. And three, you got you, the man who's gonna pull that sandblastin' hose to wherever the blaster needs it. You're the hose puller, Nolan, and you gonna keep up with all three of them blasters."

"Right," I replied. "So it's a sandblaster, a pot tender, and a hose puller."

"Right on," Richards said with a soft chuckle, patting me on the shoulder. "You're gettin' it already."

The three sandblasters stood by the barge, putting on rain gear over coveralls. They even used duct tape to seal off the cuffs on their pants and jackets, apparently to keep sand from infiltrating their clothing. Each man also tied a length of rope around his waist. I wondered why they didn't simply use a belt or a strap; later on, when I became a sandblaster, I found out why.

I glanced back at the orange sand pot, which looked like a scaled-down missile silo. The term *sand pot* didn't seem right; that concept was too small for something this imposing. Maybe *sand tower* or *sand elevator*.

The three heavy black hoses running out from the bottom of the pot were threaded through pneumatic pistons. Richards explained, "Those pistons there will clamp down tight on a hose, you know, turning it on or off." He slammed his fist in his palm for emphasis. "That pot runs at one hundred ten pounds' pressure, so you never wanna mess with those pistons. One of them blows, it'd take your head off." I nodded my understanding.

A couple electrical wires ran along each sandblast hose, and Richards pointed to them. "At the end of the hose, those cords power a floodlight and a switch to operate the piston. And at the very end, you got the nozzle."

Sandblast hose came in fifty-foot lengths. The barge we were blasting was about two hundred feet long, so each sandblaster had four lengths of hose coiled up behind him. Based on how heavy the hoses looked, I guessed that a blaster could probably wrestle about fifteen or twenty feet of hose behind him with one hand and point the nozzle with the other, so it made sense to have someone like me pulling the hose for them as they worked their way down the barge.

"You keep a ways back from them blasters," Richards ordered. "No way you wanna get hit with that sandblast. And watch out for the ricochet, too." Noting the seriousness in his tone, I would more than keep my distance.

My safety equipment this time around was not a white paper mask but a full-sized black respirator made of heavy-duty rubber, with two screw-in filters. *This looks like something from the First World War*, I thought, *something soldiers used in the trenches for mustard gas*. I fitted the respirator over my nose and mouth, fastened the straps behind my head, and screwed the twin canister filters in tight. After pulling on goggles over my safety glasses, I was ready.

The sandblasters stood under the forward end of the barge, all set to go. Richards pressurized the sand pot, the blasters turned on their hoses, and with the sound of a gathering storm, sand began to fly. In a matter of seconds, a billowing, gritty black cloud engulfed the dry dock. *It's like a sandstorm in the desert*, I told myself, *only darker and more violent*. I carefully kept my distance, and stayed at the opposite end of the angry world of sand blowing up in front of the blasters.

The sandblasters methodically worked their way aft, always aiming their nozzle toward the stern. I kept pace along with them under the barge, keeping up with the hoses but still staying a safe distance from the blasters' backs. Sandblast hose is even heavier when it's live, and sweat gathered inside my respirator and started soaking through my coveralls. From time to time I jogged back to the sand pot to check in with Richards and make sure I was doing everything correctly.

I pulled down my respirator. "So far, so good?" I asked him.

Richards just nodded. "Keep goin'."

In the midst of it all, I wanted to thank him—hell, I wanted to hug him—for not getting me fired and, even better, for taking me under his wing. I felt those emotions, but there wasn't time to find the right words, so I just kept up with the hose pulling, hoping my appreciation showed through my efforts.

One of the blasters stopped, and the hiss of the pneumatic piston cut through the air as it clamped down on his hose, cutting off the pressure. The blaster raised his arm and tapped the top of his hood three times with his gloved hand.

"That means more sand," Richards hollered, then quickly bent down and adjusted one of the valves at the bottom of the pot. The piston released, and the blaster fired back up. This was on-the-job training for me, and I was *learnin'*: the pot tender controlled how much air pressure ran through a hose and how much sand got mixed in. The blasters communicated with Richards through hand signals. When the sandblasters were not in sight of the pot tender, they communicated using their on/off switch, bumping the pneumatic piston on their hose two times for less sand, three times for more. It was just one of many tricks of the trade. Further down the road, I would understand that all the shipbuilding trades—welder, painter, ship's carpenter—looked easy to the casual observer, but each craft had hundreds of little skills and inside knowledge that, when added together, made the person who possessed them a *master craftsman.* It would take some time for me to learn the ins and outs of sandblasting, but this was a beginning, and it galvanized me.

When we broke for lunch, the only thing the other blasters said to me was "What's your name again?" I didn't try to engage in much conversation, thinking back to a college professor who had described "good students" as people with "big ears, large eyes, and *small* mouths." I kept silent. Richards, however, pulled me aside and said, "You get'n it, Nolan." My face lit up, and Richards noticed and smiled. His positive words were all I needed to hear: Richards's approval was solid gold.

The second half of the shift flew by. It was the same routine: heavy, dirty work that kept me on the run, but at the same time, I loved it. I was only a hose puller, but my participation made me a member of the sandblasting crew—I was a laborer no more. I embraced the role.

When the blasters made it down to the rear of the barge—the "ass end," as they called it—I grabbed another length of sandblast hose. Several coils were tied to a pallet sitting on the pier, and I hauled one fifty-foot length down to the blasters. All three men had shut down, and one of the guys, Eddie, removed the nozzle from the end of his hose. I helped him connect the new length of hose, watching him put in a clean gasket, then tighten the brass coupling with a metallic click. Eddie then reached in his pocket and retrieved two short pieces of copper wire, which he threaded through the coupling, a safety precaution to hold it together under pressure. As I watched all this, we never exchanged a word—his lips were clamped down on a cigarette the whole time—but I mentally recorded every detail of the process.

Eddie screwed on the nozzle, then blasted the remaining area as the shift wound down, the job completed. Minutes later, I was back in the locker room, washing up. In the mirror over the sink, I stared at a perfect outline of the respirator and goggles etched in black sand on my face, raccoon-like, and I started laughing. The whistle blew to signal the end of the shift. No one said anything about me coming back tomorrow, but what the hell—no one gave me a pink slip either.

Ten minutes later I was in line to punch my timecard. I noticed the two scalers I'd started the shift with, which seemed like a long time ago, and one joked, "Yo, mister sand man," with a grin.

The other guy added, "It's the master blaster...the guy with all the experience. You do okay, Nolan?"

I relaxed. "Yeah, no problem" was my breezy reply, as if I'd been blasting for years. They were both holding pink slips with their timecards, and I suddenly felt a trace of Catholic guilt because I'd lied to get the job.

It was obvious, though, that these guys didn't care. One of them picked up on me noticing the pink slips and laughed. "Yeah...we both got riffed."

The other guy nodded. "I was looking for a job when I got here, and I'll be looking for a job when I leave."

I laughed too. The three of us clocked out and dropped our timecards in the slot, then said so long and went our separate ways, never to see each other again.

The next afternoon I bussed back to Lockheed Yard Two at 4:00 for swing shift. As I walked through the gate, I almost expected someone to grab the timecard out of my hand and say, "What the hell are you doing here? You were supposed to be laid off last night!" Instead, I moved with the incoming crowd and punched my card like everyone else. The grin on my face reflected the irony of my circumstances. For four years I had been the quintessential rule follower. Compliance—and honesty—were considered virtues. But the fact was, I didn't get ahead until I started lying about myself. This wasn't turning out the way I expected, but I had to admit it was working.

I made my way down to the dry dock, where I was welcomed with a friendly wave from Richards. "Back for more, huh?" He smiled. "You done good yesterday, Nolan."

The three sandblasters made their way down the pier to join us and ask, “What’s your name again?”

“Nolan.”

“Oh yeah…that’s right.”

I immediately felt a connection to Richards, who was magnanimous and sympathetic to my situation, and if the other guys didn’t say much, at least they accepted me. They *must* have noticed how hard I worked yesterday. Although I had only worked in the shipyard a short time, it was long enough for me to understand one of the unspoken truths of the blue-collar world: putting in a hard day’s work gets noticed. No matter your age, race, or experience, if you bust your ass in heavy construction, you earn a degree of respect.

Richards waved me over to get things started. “Today we doin’ the upper hull. Espy, you take the starboard side. Dunbar can pull hose for ya. Nolan, you go with Eddie down the port side.”

Now I knew everybody’s name. Looking up at the barge, I could see where the day shift had painted the area we blasted last night. The entire bottom of the hull was now a dull red, and the new paint continued just a little bit up the sides of the barge. Today we would blast the rest of the way up the hull. The area was too high to reach standing on the dry dock, so the sandblasters would work in man-lifts: four-wheeled vehicles with an extendable boom holding a basket and a dashboard of controls. There were two of these vehicles parked on the dry dock: one on the port side, the other on the starboard side.

Eddie and Espy climbed into the man-lifts. Once an area was blasted, they would shut down their hoses, move the man-lift a little farther down the hull, then fire up again, repeating this process over and over until they reached the ass end.

With the spray always directed to the stern, Eddie and Espy maneuvered their vehicles through the narrow space between the hull and the towering side of the dry dock, called the “wing wall.” Hose-pulling in this situation was easy: the hose was tied to the side of the basket, and when the man-lift was driven down the dry dock, the hose was pulled along with it. Eddie told me, “Just make sure the dragging hose don’t knock something over or get hung up while I’m moving.”

“Got it,” I said.

The first half of the shift went by without a hitch, and when we broke for lunch, Eddie hopped down from the man-lift, took me aside, and said,

"You're doing good, Nolan, real good." That was music to my ears. And his words confirmed that I was becoming one of the crew.

The other guys joined us as Eddie lit up a cigarette. "The first rule of driving that man-lift," Eddie told me, "is don't drive off the end of the fucking dry dock."

Dunbar joined in. "You remember the time ol' Jesse done that?"

"Sure do," Eddie answered. "That motherfucker was drunk."

"I think the white hat on duty done *shit his dress* when he saw that man-lift go over the side." Espy chuckled.

"Yeah...I remember that white hat," Dunbar said. "He got on the emergency dock phone and called the production manager after the man-lift was in the drink. He says, 'I got some good news and I got some bad news. The good news is, the scuba divers are already on the way.'" Dunbar slapped his leg, and everyone laughed.

We finished the blasting before the end of the shift and spent the last half-hour coiling up the hoses on pallets and shoveling the spent sand—a truckload of it—off the end of the dry dock and into the bay. There was just enough time for another smoke as our shift wound down, and that's when the swing-shift white hat came walking our way down the pier.

He stuck his hands in his pockets and looked at us. "Good work tonight, guys." Turning to the other scalers, he said, "You four will be moving to that monster over there tomorrow." He nodded to the ship moored at the next pier, then turned his attention to me and said the magic words. "Nolan, you'll be going to day shift. Report to the AS39 tomorrow morning. Garcia will be your leadman."

I nodded as a smile spread over my face. The AS39, the USS *Emory Land*, was a submarine tender, a mammoth Navy vessel being built in *new construction.*

Seniority, here I come.

CHAPTER 7

I punched my timecard the next morning convinced I was entering the land of milk and honey. Ahead of me lay work in new construction. *I will enjoy an uninterrupted job, go to work at the same location every day, and get a paycheck each Friday.* I took a deep breath. *Best of all, I won't get laid off anymore.*

Some of those things came true.

My energetic steps carried me up the creaky wooden stairs to the men's locker room, but as I entered, I still felt like a stranger. It was crowded but there weren't any ship scalers I recognized. I sat by myself at one of the long wooden tables until the whistle blew, and the guys around me finished the last of their coffee and stowed their lunch pails.

Trying to look as though I belonged, I jumped into the crowd flowing down the steps and into the main yard, one among hundreds of workers on their way to various ships. My eyes were drawn to the cloudless blue sky, where gulls wheeled and called overhead. The salty air tasted crisp and fresh as I stopped to take a deep breath. *What a glorious morning.*

I had no problem figuring out where to go. The *Emory Land*, a massive haze-gray Navy ship with "39" painted on her bow in oversized block numbers, was easy to spot. Her sister ship, the AS40 *Frank Cable*, was in an earlier stage of construction and moored opposite her. Beyond the ships lay Elliott Bay, and to the east I could see the skyline of downtown Seattle, all steel and glass, illuminated in the morning sun. I stopped once more to take it all in, then joined the workers streaming up the long gangway to the main deck of the AS39.

This is it. I gripped the railing, all nervous energy, as a little kid's anxious smile parted my lips.

The main deck was like Grand Central Station, a chaotic, noisy procession of workers all wearing different-colored hard hats, everyone in a hurry and moving in all directions. Halfway across the deck stood a short, fidgety man with pale blue eyes, close-cropped white hair, and a trim white mustache. His orange hard hat was marked with a capital F.

"You the scaler foreman?" I asked, handing him my timecard.

"That's right," he said. "Oh yeah...Nolan. You're on Garcia's crew. They're in the head, aft of the galley." He handed my timecard back. "Follow me."

The foreman's name was Hildebrand, but everyone referred to him as "the Warden." Though he was an older man, Hildebrand was solid and tough and quick, and always on the move. His clipped, precise speech matched his movements as he directed me below deck with the occasional "This way" and "Over here" and "Come on" tossed over his shoulder.

I followed the Warden down two levels to the ship's galley, which was currently serving as a sprawling office space for white hats. Galley tables had been papered over and set up as makeshift desks, cluttered with blueprints and work orders and construction plans. Aft of this workspace was a giant industrial kitchen, and beyond that was a large head, or latrine.

"Hildebrand!" one of the white hats barked. The Warden stopped and pointed me in the direction of the head. "Right over there, Nolan. Look for Garcia." Then he turned back to the white hat.

Inside the head, two electricians were connecting a string of overhead lights, and six scalers worked hunched under a row of sinks, cleaning pipes. *This must be my new crew, so where is the leadman?*

A middle-aged woman in gray coveralls stood in one corner, leaning against the bulkhead with her arms folded across her chest. Under her hard hat I could see bleached-blonde hair pulled back into a bun, and a blue bandana wrapped tight around her head, straining her features into a severe mask.

"Do you know where I can find Garcia?" I asked her.

She scowled at me and spat out, "Gimme your timecard!"

Intimidated, I handed over my timecard as commanded. She glared at it, then shouted, "Well, don't just stand there. Get down with the rest of the crew and clean those pipes." She pointed to an open spot underneath the counter. I grabbed a pair of heavy rubber gloves, a wire brush, and some rags from a cardboard box on the floor, then bent down and began to copy the work everyone else was doing.

Next to me was a younger guy: a trim, angular man with a pencil-thin mustache. He cleaned a drainpipe as a cigarette dangled from his lips. Looking up, he smiled. "Welcome to paradise. What's your name, anyway?"

I got as far as "No—" when Garcia cut me off with a sharp "Get to work! If you want to ask him for a date, Nolan, do it on your own time."

The scalers under the counter all looked at each other and broke up laughing as I crouched down and got busy cleaning pipes. "Somebody get him some paint stripper," Garcia yelled to no one in particular.

The guy next to me, whose name was Lamar, stood up and grabbed a can of stripper, then set it down between us. "Keep your gloves on and watch this stuff," Lamar said under his breath, without looking away from his work. The stripper was an opaque, viscous substance, not a solid but not exactly a liquid either. "You don't want to get any on your skin."

He was right. I wore rubber gloves, but a little fleck landed on my upper arm and burned instantly. I quickly rolled my sleeves down and adjusted my safety glasses. Several of the scalers also protected their faces with bandanas, Billy the Kid style.

On the other side was a woman named Esther, who now said, "Yeah… this here is powerful stuff." I put a blob of stripper on the pipe with a small brush and watched it curdle the paint. After I rubbed it in with a wire brush and wiped it, the fitting sparkled. The only problem was that the wire brush tended to kick little globs of stripper back at me if I wasn't careful. I felt a little spot on my chin, then one on my cheek, burn. Thank god for safety glasses.

Garcia paced behind us, looking over our work. This group of six scalers seemed different from other crews I had worked with. For one thing, it was more diverse: counting me, the crew included three Whites and three Blacks, and two of the scalers were women. The other difference was that, right from the start, I felt tension in this group. Of the crews I had been on before, I always sensed an easygoing, laid-back esprit de corps. Not here. Garcia's crew was all work and no play. In a half-hour, the silver pipes under the counter were cleaned and shined to perfection.

"I can see your reflection, Nolan," Esther said with a grin.

"Garcia to the second-deck mike!" rang overhead, interrupting us. I recognized the Warden's voice. "On the double!" Our leadman was being summoned to the broadcast microphone located on the second deck.

"Stay here and keep working" were Garcia's parting words.

The moment our leadman left, everything changed. The crew relaxed, stopped what they were doing, and started talking. Lamar lit another cigarette and leaned back on the deck on one elbow. "So, you decided to come and work for Garcia, huh?"

"I just want to be in new construction. I need to get my seniority…I was slowly dying being laid off all the time in ship repair."

"Yeah…" Lamar nodded. "I'm glad they sent me to new construction, too. I just wish they hadn't sent me to Carol. But she's our leadman, the one and only Carol Garcia." Despite the faded coveralls and scuffed steel-toe work boots, Lamar had a dignified air about him, a presence. He had class.

"This here crew got put together in June," Esther said. "It's the same group 'cept for two guys who Carol decided she didn't like. She got rid of 'em."

"They were okay," Lamar said. "They just couldn't stand Carol, and she knew it, so she figured out a way to get them laid off."

The crew went silent for a moment, then Lamar tilted his head back and blew a stream of cigarette smoke. "I was looking for a job when I got here, and I'll be looking for a job when I leave."

"Amen to that..." one of the scalers said, as others nodded in agreement.

"She's coming," Esther said, getting the words out just in time. Everyone immediately went back to work.

Carol walked into the compartment and put her hands on her hips. "Pack up your gear, everyone. We're heading down a couple levels to do some deck grinding. Lamar, you and Hawkins go to the tool room and get five deck grinders and two needle guns. Everyone else, come with me."

We grabbed our equipment and followed Carol out of the compartment as she yelled at Lamar over her shoulder, "And pick up a box of those paper masks too. Meet us at 3-25-4."

That was another bit of shipyard terminology I didn't understand yet, but Esther clued me in. "All compartments are numbered, Nolan. That's how you find your way 'round. Every passageway, every space on the ship, got its own number. It's a system all the ships use, so a person can find their way around on any big ship. Don't matter if they've never been on board before."

Esther explained that a person could find their way to a specific place by following the numbers. "Carol saying '3-25-4'," she explained, "means Lamar can find us by starting at the main deck and going down, below decks, to the third level. That's the 'three.' Then he could count the frames—you know, the bulkheads—from the bow all the way goin' aft and find us at the twenty-fifth one. That's the 'twenty-five.' And from the twenty-fifth bulkhead," Esther continued, "Lamar can find us in the fourth compartment over, on the port side. Even numbered compartments on the port side, odd numbers on starboard." Once I understood the system, it was a breeze finding my way around the ship. Carol led the crew down to the third deck and our new worksite: an empty, unfinished compartment with cables and wiring running overhead through brackets, the wiring looking like stretched-out bunches of spaghetti. A string of lights hung from the center of the overhead, as well as a ventilation hose.

Entering the compartment, Esther looked at the deck, then back at me. "We'll be gettin' this here ready for the painters." With the toe of her work boot, she kicked at amber patches that speckled the deck. "That's where the deck grinders and the needle guns gonna get used."

Lamar and Hawkins came back with the tools and a bunch of air hoses, and Carol glanced over her shoulder. "Okay…let's rig those hoses up and get things going."

A stocky middle-aged ship scaler named Bob grabbed a deck grinder and hose, attached them to a long brass manifold just outside the compartment, and tested it with a couple quick pulls of the trigger. Satisfied, he strapped on a paper respirator, adjusted his safety glasses, then dropped to his knees and started grinding away at the rust spots.

The other scalers did the same with deck grinders and needle guns, which were used to clean corners and tight spaces the deck grinders couldn't reach. Everyone wore paper respirator masks, because even with the ventilation hose sucking air from the compartment, the space quickly became cloudy with a mixture of ground paint, steel, and rust. The sound created by seven people running high-pressure pneumatic tools in a confined, steel-sided space was deafening, even with earplugs.

We finished grinding the deck before the lunch break and spent the last few minutes sweeping out the compartment. I stood and stretched my back, taking off my respirator. "Gross," I said to no one. The white paper respirator had turned a dull red brown. The whistle blew, and everyone set down their brooms and dustpans before filing out of the ship and onto the pier.

I walked across the yard toward the men's locker room, then headed up the old wooden staircase and managed to find the locker where I'd stashed my lunch pail and thermos.

Hands down, the best lunch was always the one I brought from home. There were only two other options: vending machines, where you could buy a bag of chips or a candy bar, or the "gut wagon," which sold hot food. This was long before fresh food trucks invaded Seattle. The gut wagon bore almost no similarity to those, offering precooked cheeseburgers, burritos, and corndogs wrapped in plastic and steam-heated in the back of the truck. "Food as a last resort" was how Lamar described it. I had tried a couple burritos once, and they turned to lead in my gut. From then on, I forced myself to get up early enough to make a proper lunch. Over time I became adept at creating oversized meat-and-cheese deli sandwiches.

I took my lunch pail and sat down at one of the long wooden tables. The room was a little hazy, because a lot of men liked to have a cigarette with their coffee after eating. I settled into the cozy, slightly cloudy atmosphere.

I could tell by the conversation that the same people ate lunch together every day. I didn't see Lamar or Bob, but there were places other than the locker room to eat. Some people favored the tables next to the vending machines by the tool room, and others sat outside, leaning up against the building or a stack of pallets on the pier, especially when the weather was nice. I didn't know the people I sat down with, but I joined in the conversation.

Before long, the whistle blew, and I stowed my lunch pail and filed down the stairs with the rest of the guys, ambling out into the yard. Remembering "3-25-4," I managed to find my way back to our worksite without getting turned around, thanks to Esther explaining the system to me. The AS39 was six hundred feet long and built for a crew of 1,300, so being aboard ship felt like working in a busy downtown office building, one with so many floors and similar-looking spaces that you could get lost if you didn't know the system.

The rest of the afternoon was spent deck grinding, and the crew knocked out three compartments before the end of the shift. We had just moved to the fourth when Carol gathered us together and handed out timecards. "Stow your tools there in the corner. Meet me on the weather deck tomorrow morning."

That was it. "Okay," I told myself, "I made it through my first day in new construction. I'm gonna get my seniority." My worries were over, or so I thought.

CHAPTER 8

The next few weeks were a carbon copy of that first day in new construction. Each morning, I joined hundreds of workers striding up the long aluminum gangway to the main deck of the AS39: "walking the plank," as Lamar put it. Our crew of ship scalers would start the shift on the main deck, gathering around Carol Garcia, handing her our timecards, and following her to a worksite somewhere on the ship. The crew was assigned various cleanup projects from time to time but most of the work involved deck grinding.

Everyone dressed in coveralls, and all of us wore respirators and safety earmuffs; most of the crew also put on goggles over their safety glasses. The dust that resulted from eight hours of deck grinding was insidious, creeping into any little opening in our clothing and dirtying any exposed sliver of skin, so we bundled up. Only Carol was able to keep her clothes clean. Her job as leadman was to direct the work, not pick up a tool. That was a union rule. The agreement with the company specified a leadman or foreman could supervise a worker but not take their place.

I loved the union because it got me my job, but I wondered if that particular rule worked against the company and maybe, over time, against the union itself. On the other hand, if someone decided that *I* should become a leadman, I wouldn't complain about not working.

Carol stood stiffly in the corner of the compartment, arms crossed, watching over us with harsh eyes—all part of her icy demeanor. *What's the deal?* I wondered, glancing over at her. *Why is she like that?* It didn't make sense, considering the work we were getting done. The crew was cooperative, always on the job, constantly in motion. In fact, the only time I actually stood still and looked at Carol Garcia was in the morning, when I gave her my timecard. Looking closely, I could see that she wore heavy makeup, with penciled-on eyebrows and a penciled mole on her cheek, like Marilyn Monroe. I could tell the mole was drawn because, after two weeks on Carol's crew, I noticed it wasn't always in the same spot. Her abrasive personality, however, never varied.

I thought of Carol as a "dura mater," which is Latin for "hard mother." One morning while I followed her below deck, we walked past a tall, dignified-looking white hat standing by a bulkhead with his hands in his coverall pockets. "That cocksucker owes me twenty-five dollars," Carol said under her breath as we passed by. A little farther down the passageway, she added, "Look at that son of a bitch standing there, playing pocket pool."

I accepted Carol's negativity toward white hats, but I couldn't figure out why she was down on her own crew—especially Bob, who was the least likely guy to offend anyone, much less say anything back. A congenial, if simple, person, Bob didn't deserve the "Don't just stand there playing with yourself. Get to work!" type of comments that Carol would throw his way. I never said anything about it, because something inside held me back. Instead I'd stew, often coming up with the perfect response ten minutes later. Looking back, I should have spoken up, but I kept my head down and stayed busy. After all, I didn't want Carol's vitriol to be directed at me.

As the days went by, I fell into the rhythm of work, becoming comfortable with the job and with the other scalers, if not with the leadman. As a crew we typically worked together at the same site, but every once in a while, an individual would get detailed out to a different job. The most common assignment was as a "fire watch" for a welder, a job some scalers liked but which I found excruciatingly boring and tried my best to avoid.

Welders make a lot of sparks while working, occasionally igniting things around them or igniting themselves without even noticing. The risk of self-immolation was kept down by the welder's heavy leather gloves, a leather jacket, and a leather apron or chaps. Nearby flammable objects were covered in Refrasil, a shiny orange fire-resistant fabric. As an additional precaution, a ship scaler was assigned to stand next to the welder, holding a fire extinguisher, watching for anything to catch fire.

I remember eight-hour shifts as a fire watch when I never once put out anything with my fire extinguisher. I had stretches when the only time my fire extinguisher was used was when someone wanted to spray their can of Dr. Pepper to cool it off for lunch. Yes, it works. A fire extinguisher is handy for that.

After three or four weeks on Carol's crew, a detail for a separate job came my way. The white hat in charge of shipyard recycling was an overweight, sweaty, nearsighted man named Rivers whose bad dental hygiene earned him the nickname "Old Green Teeth." One day Rivers approached the Warden saying he needed a scaler to scour the yard with him and gather up cardboard to be recycled, so for three days, I was detailed as his crew of one.

Machinery was delivered to the shipyard in oversized, thick cardboard boxes, usually arriving strapped to a wooden pallet. A worker would cut the straps, slice the cardboard, and take the machinery, leaving the cardboard scattered on the pier or on the ship's deck for someone else to clean up. Management at Lockheed must have figured out a way to make a buck recycling the cardboard, because Rivers and I searched each deck on every ship, retrieving boxes and cut-up pieces of cardboard, some of them bigger than me. Old Green Teeth had a couple "dinos"—freight-car-sized dumpsters—set aside specifically for cardboard, and it was my job to fill them up.

Rivers might have been odd-looking, and yes, he had crummy teeth, but he was easygoing, and working for him was a breath of fresh air after struggling through all the free-floating tension that permeated Carol's crew. I could have spent three weeks happily gathering cardboard for Rivers, but after three days we had eradicated cardboard from Lockheed Shipyard and Rivers sent me back to Carol Garcia.

The next morning found me on the main deck of the AS39, reluctantly handing my timecard to Carol but also glad to be checking in with my buddies on the crew.

"Welcome back, Nolan," Bob said.

"Old Green Teeth treat you okay?" Lamar asked, adding with a sardonic smile, "Lemme guess…you just couldn't stay away from your girlfriend Carol, right?" His grin got even wider when he quietly added, "It's okay, Nolan, you can tell me." He nudged me in the ribs and whispered, "Your secret is safe with me."

Esther overheard us and started laughing. "Oh, go on!"

I rolled my eyes as we all followed Carol to the worksite and got busy grinding decks again. At this point deck grinding had become monotonous, but the boredom was weighed against a fat weekly paycheck. Every Friday morning I'd line up in the drafty auditorium-like space below the men's locker room to get paid. Besides the tool room and some vending machines and picnic tables down there, there were seven or eight bank teller windows, divided up alphabetically. I'd show my work badge to the teller, and she'd hand me my paycheck.

I made good money. In 1978, the minimum wage in the state of Washington was $2.65 an hour. Lockheed Shipyard paid $10.50 an hour when I started, and that rose to $13.50 by the time I left, five years later. Overtime paid double that rate, and since we had paid holidays, working on a holiday equaled triple time. As one grizzled welder explained to me, "We got 'em by the shorthairs on weekends and holidays. When a vessel limps into ship repair, it makes no difference to the ship's owner if it's a holiday." He grinned like a pirate. "They gotta have the work done right then, so they pay whatever it takes."

The union drove a hard bargain with the shipyards to get me that wage, as well as medical and dental covered at one hundred percent, and I was thankful. All of the shipyard workers—the welders, joiners, painters, machinists, and all of the trade crafts—bargained as a single entity under one umbrella, known as the Joint Metal Trades Council, affiliated with the AFL-CIO. The people holding that umbrella had leverage, because crafts down the West Coast stuck together and were willing to strike to support one another. There really was strength in numbers.

The part that floored me was that everyone working in the shipyard got the same wage. A ship scaler pushing a broom was taking home the same pay as an electrician or a machinist or a boilermaker. No offense to the scaler pushing the broom—someone's got to do it—but the difference in skill level was night and day. If Lockheed Shipyard agreed to pay me, the guy hired on as a laborer, the same wage as a journeyman electrician—*are you kidding?*—I wasn't going to complain. On the other hand, a little voice in the back of my head said, *This can't go on forever.* And it didn't. But at the time, I happily collected my paycheck on Friday morning along with everyone else.

Our crew continued to perform deck-grinding jobs interspersed with cleanup work. We were also assigned to follow up in areas that had been sandblasted—spaces with an inch or more of sand on the deck—and get them ready for the painters. We did that cleaning using a sandblast hose that the pot tender had reversed the pressure on, creating the world's most powerful vacuum cleaner. The first time I wrestled with that vacuum hose, my initial impulse was to hold it straight down, but it was impossible to keep the hose from suddenly adhering to the deck with a loud *thunk*, after which I struggled to pry it loose. I had to use both hands and carefully hold the hose at an angle to get the work done.

The vacuum inhaled sand, pieces of welding rod, nuts and bolts—anything in its path. More than once the hose sucked the glove off my hand, all in the blink of an eye. One time, just for a second, I lost my grip, and as I fumbled for the hose—*thunk!*—it stuck to my right thigh, and I had to yank it free from my pant leg. That night after work, taking a shower at my apartment, I laughed when I noticed the world's biggest hickey on my thigh, staring at me like a cyclops.

At this point I knew my way around the shipyard and felt a sense of camaraderie with the other scalers on the crew. The rules of the game were to do exactly what Carol told you to do, without asking questions. And when she gave you grief, the rules said to go with the flow, keep your head down, and stay busy. The Warden passed by a couple times each day but never said much. Hildebrand came across as a tough old-timer, but I wondered if, underneath it all, he was just as intimidated by Carol as the rest of us.

I knew nothing about Carol personally, other than she was married once. I'd overheard part of a conversation she had with Esther one day. "Yeah, I met him after he enlisted in the Navy," Carol said of her Filipino husband. "We were married for twelve years, then the son of a bitch up and died on me." At that point, I clapped on my industrial earmuffs and focused on the work in front of me.

I became proficient with both needle gun and deck grinder. A pneumatic grinder is fitted with a round abrasive disc, the surface of which is rougher than the coarsest sandpaper you can imagine. Even so, the grit on the disc eventually wears down and the grinder needs to be fitted with a new disc, a few of which I carried with me.

Once, when all of us were grinding away, Bob ran out of discs. Setting down his grinder, he walked over to me. "Nolan, you got an extra disc?"

"Quit dicking around and get back to work!" Carol hollered across the room. "We're trying to get this compartment ready, and you two are playing grab ass!"

Neither Bob nor I responded to her. Turning away from Carol, I handed Bob the new disc and said under my breath, "She's crazy. This place is crazy." Bob put his mask back on and shrugged.

I shook my head. "What am I doing here?"

Bob pulled his mask back down. "Earning a paycheck." We kept working.

It got worse. A week later, the crew was working in the ship's superstructure, picking up trash just outside a space called the CIC—the Combat Information Center. Packing material was scattered everywhere: oddly-shaped pieces of thick Styrofoam; plastic wrap; and five-foot-long, four-inch-thick flexible Styrofoam tubes. After being instructed to "clean this shit up," we began stuffing the Styrofoam and other trash into plastic garbage bags, but the long tubes were too big and ungainly for the bags.

Bob grabbed five or six Styrofoam tubes in a bear hug and was walking them down to a dumpster when Carol stepped behind him and said, "I think

I'll take one of those and shove it up my pussy. Then I can walk around with a big smile on my face."

I couldn't believe what I was hearing, but everyone laughed. Lamar, who was working next to me, shot me a sidelong glance and said under his breath, "Leastways she'll be smilin'."

When the laughter stopped, Carol added, "No…I better not. If I shoved that in and walked down the ladder, I'd probably have my period."

Again, everyone burst out laughing. This was, after all, a shipyard, and this was "shipyard humor." It was also the late 1970s, years before sexual harassment in the workplace was commonly identified as a problem. All that considered, the whole exchange gave me a lousy feeling. Once more, I asked myself what I was doing here.

It wasn't only Carol's language; after a couple months on the job, I'd become desensitized to hearing the word *fuck* three times in every sentence. Crude and vulgar dialogue was expected in a shipyard. What bothered me was Carol's eagerness to use her words against us like a club. I was sick of listening to the never-ending put-downs. I was getting clubbed to death. *God knows why she does it*, I thought, shaking my head, *but she's damn good at it. Too good…in the worst kind of way.*

I shrugged my shoulders, exchanged an exasperated look with Lamar, and kept picking up trash. I didn't say anything. No one did. The crew eventually lugged all the garbage bags, as well as the smile-inducing Styrofoam tubes, down to the main deck and tossed them into a battered blue dumpster.

I looked out over the water. Elliott Bay seemed as big as the ocean right then, and my mind drifted over the surface. Was the tide bringing me in or taking me away? *Do I belong here? How much do I need this job? How much do I want this job?* I could feel the pull of the tide, but I wasn't sure which direction it was taking me.

Thinking back now, I have to admit that some of my reaction to Carol was a reflection of how young I was, how green I was, how totally unschooled I was in the hard realities of rough work and even rougher people. I didn't know when or how to let things slide. I was still the new guy, the young college kid wandering in a strange, foreign land.

At the time, though, it all started to bother me, and I became conflicted about keeping the job. The tide was pulling harder on me now, and I sensed it might be pulling me right out of the shipyard.

CHAPTER 9

The nail in the coffin came a week later. The crew was on another cleanup job, this time on the main deck, also called the weather deck. Two scalers stacked empty pallets off to one side while the rest of us picked up rope, packing tape, and plastic sheeting and tossed it into a dumpster. I came across some oversized pieces of cardboard and thought of Old Green Teeth and his recycling project. There was still a giant dino for recycled cardboard at the end of the pier.

I stopped and asked Carol, "Do you want me to haul this cardboard down the pier to the dino instead of tossing it in the dumpster?"

She looked at me as if I were crazy. "Jesus fucking Christ, no!" she bellowed. "Just throw it in the goddamn dumpster!"

My jaw tightened, but I kept my mouth shut and turned away from her, tossing the cardboard into the dumpster.

Carol snuck up behind me and barked, "Any idiot could figure that out!"

I whipped around and met her stare, saying through clenched teeth, "Now wait a minute..."

She stepped closer until we were nose to nose, then yelled even louder, "ANY IDIOT COULD FIGURE THAT OUT!"

I was on the ropes, but instead of fighting back, I hesitated, and my indecision killed me.

"Now get to work!" Carol turned and walked away.

I stood there fuming. *That does it. I'm done. I'm outta here.* Like a silent robot, I mechanically picked up trash, but storms howled inside me. Both Esther and Lamar saw what happened and tried to talk to me, but I was beyond words. I finished the shift in silence and stayed that way on the bus ride home. *I'm not gonna keep doing this*, I repeated to myself, shaking my head.

That evening, alone in my apartment, I couldn't get the episode off my mind. My thoughts kept going back and forth. Here I was, in new construction, *the land of milk and honey*, and now I was going to quit.

I hate this job.

I'd finally earned my seniority, was making a steady wage, and had job security. *I can't walk away from that.*

Exasperation was getting me nowhere; I needed to make a decision. By the time I went to bed, I had settled on *No job is worth this much grief, no matter how much I'm getting paid.*

The confrontation with Carol took place on a Monday in late November. Riding the bus to work Tuesday morning, I resolved to quit at the end of the shift. I'd find Hildebrand when the whistle blew and tell him I was done. It's just like they say: *I was looking for a job when I got here, and I'll be looking for a job when I leave.*

Coming to that decision settled me, but there was one other factor to consider: Thanksgiving was the day after tomorrow, and the concept of a *paid* holiday, actually earning money for a day I didn't work, was still new to me and incredibly appealing. *You must be kidding me...you mean they pay us even when we don't work?*

I went back to bargaining with myself, finally deciding I could put up with Carol until the end of the week for an extra day's pay. I would endure Tuesday and Wednesday, come back after Thanksgiving, then work the Friday shift and tell the Warden I quit.

Completing my game plan finally brought peace of mind. I worked the two days, and when the whistle blew Wednesday afternoon, I went back to my apartment and packed an overnight bag. After catching the bus downtown, I walked through the Pike Place Market, past the fishmongers, and down to the ferry terminal.

My dad met me at the Bainbridge Island ferry landing. Seeing my dad banished my Carol Garcia thoughts, or at least pushed them to the deep recesses of my mind. He grabbed my bag and we shook hands. As I stood beside him, everything was okay again.

"How's the big city treating you?" he asked.

"Good," I lied, not wanting to lose that easy feeling I got from being around him.

Dad tossed his arm over my shoulder and smiled. "We have a real feast ready for you at home. Mom made three different pies." He stopped and did something he wouldn't usually do: pulled me in close with his other arm and gave me a hug. "You know...I'm proud of you for making that job at Lockheed work out. From what Nancy tells me, the job market in the city is fierce, and on top of that, I hear it's pretty rough and tumble in the shipyard." There was genuine admiration in his voice.

A lump formed in my throat. "You could say that." I looked away and took a deep breath. "Tell me everything that's new at home."

The familiar drive, and my dad talking about family, centered me. The sound of his voice and the passing scenery blended together, and thoughts of Lockheed Shipyard, idiots, cardboard, Styrofoam tubes, and quitting my job faded away. As soon as we arrived home, the warmth of my family enveloped me. I slept in my old bed that night and woke up Thanksgiving morning refreshed and clearheaded, easily shifting gears to the festive holiday mood.

Everyone wanted to hear stories about me working in the shipyard. My family was an attentive audience, and I have to admit that having all eyes focused on me at dinner prompted some swagger in my storytelling. I had everyone on the edge of their seats for the one about camping out at midnight in front of the union hall, sleeping on the sidewalk, and being confronted by the cop. My description of scraping the underside of the barge while dead sealife fell on me didn't need any embellishment: they loved that one, too. I left out the story about Carol, the long Styrofoam tubes, and where she was going to shove them. I also didn't mention her calling me an idiot.

"So you like being a ship scaler?" Dad asked, leaning back in his chair.

I hesitated for a second, then grinned. "I like the paycheck." What I wanted to say was "I don't think anyone actually *likes* being a ship scaler," but that didn't fit in with my stories.

Of all the family gathered that Thanksgiving, one person, Vinny, understood my situation through firsthand experience. Vinny was married to my other sister and, as a construction worker himself, had comparable stories of his own. When I told my tales at dinner, Vinny didn't comment, but he smiled knowingly.

At six foot two and well over two hundred pounds, Vinny was built like a tank. He had lank shoulder-length hair and a droopy Fu Manchu mustache, and you could tell he had never attended charm school. Vinny cut a dominating, commanding figure—his favorite pastime was riding a gigantic Harley: his *hog*, as he called it.

Vinny belonged to the Hod Carriers Union, the building industry's equivalent of the Ship Scalers Union, both representing laborers. A "hod" is two boards nailed together, one perpendicular to the other, with a handle mounted underneath. It's cut to fit on a person's shoulder and used to haul bricks or mortar to a bricklayer.

Vinny had been a hod carrier for several years, and his arms were as thick as my legs. If you didn't know the guy, you might keep your distance, based on his looks. The surprising thing was, underneath the intimidating exterior, Vinny had a big, generous heart and possessed a terrific sense of humor. Still, I'd never want to cross the guy.

After recounting enough shipyard tales to satisfy my family during dinner, I found myself out on the deck with Vinny, both of us nursing a beer. When I confided in him about the stories I had left out—about Carol Garcia—he nodded.

"Yeah…I had a foreman at a building site who was like that. A real prick, just like what you described." Vinny sighed and shook his head. "He was giving me shit all the time, and I finally got fed up with it."

I grinned. "So you punched his lights out?" It wouldn't have been the first time. We both took another sip of beer, and it was Vinny's turn to smile.

"No, I wanted to *keep* that job." We drank a little more. "I found something else that worked." Vinny looked down at the ground for a second and grinned. "Every time that foreman started to ride my ass, I'd stop what I was doing, stand there, and say, 'Yeah…yeah…yeah.' And if he kept at it, I'd stay where I was and say it louder, 'YEAH…YEAH…YEAH.'" Vinny recounted this with a serious look on his face, then broke out laughing. "It worked, too. The son of a bitch left me alone after that."

"You didn't splatter his nose all over his face?"

"Didn't need to."

"And you didn't get fired?"

"Oh, hell no."

It was getting late, and my dad drove me back to the ferry. The drive was quiet, but in a good way. I needed the early evening stillness and the low hum of the car to sort things out in my head.

Thinking about dinner, and when Dad asked me how I liked work, my first thought was no one actually liked working in a place like the shipyard, but that wasn't totally accurate. I *did* like working at Lockheed. Not the ship scaling work itself: it was dirty, loud, tiring, and mind-numbingly repetitive. What I liked—up until now, at least—was that I had stuck with a challenging situation in a setting I had no familiarity with, and made it work.

Even better, working in heavy construction had given me an identity. I knew it was a stereotype, but I embraced the mythology that, as a hard-hat guy, I possessed a certain level of strength and toughness and competence.

The average person didn't work blue-collar construction, but in my mind, people recognized the work as clearing some sort of bar, like earning your Eagle Scout or making it through boot camp. A construction worker, by definition, was a force to be reckoned with, someone you could count on to get the job done. How could that not be appealing to a guy who had spent four years with his nose in the books? My occupation made me over. I'd worked hard and found success in the shipyard, and I took pride in that. I was a construction worker, a ship scaler, and, for the first time since graduation, I felt good about myself.

On Tuesday, I'd resolved to quit my job. Now, two days later, I was being won over by growing thoughts of confidence. Vinny's pep talk was more than just advice; his story provided a bigger picture that brought my circumstances into focus. I didn't kid myself into thinking I could be the next Vinny, but I had it in me to at least confront Carol. I could make this work.

Dad and I arrived at the ferry terminal, and I shook his hand and thanked him. I even put my arm around Dad's shoulder, which was about as close as I usually came to expressing something personal and emotional with him. I loved my dad and felt tremendous respect and affection for him, but I didn't have any practice with the words to convey those feelings.

Sailing on the ferry across Elliott Bay to downtown, I looked to the south and saw the cranes and dry docks of the shipyard. I nodded, thinking everything at Lockheed could be sorted out. It was possible. Vinny was my coach, my patron saint, and he was pointing the way forward. I just needed to follow. I nodded again and repeated, "Yeah, yeah, yeah," under my breath.

CHAPTER 10

On the bus to work Friday morning, I silently practiced Vinny's lines and thought about the psychology behind his strategy. Confronting a person like Carol involved fear. Mine, not hers, because the woman was fearless. I needed to see my fear, recognize it, and try to understand it. Then I could decide what to do about it.

So what was I afraid of? Being humiliated in front of my coworkers? Getting fired? I *would* be humiliated and maybe even fired, but I reminded myself I was prepared to quit anyway, so what the hell? I was in charge of the situation. It was *my* decision. Straightening my shoulders, I held my head just a little higher, satisfied in figuring this much out. Believe it or not, that simple bit of analysis was enough to empower me.

I was primed to flex my newfound "confidence muscle" the next time Carol rode me. The funny thing was, as the day progressed, Carol never once got on my back. It probably helped that we were working down in the machine room, where the noise level made conversation all but impossible. Everyone on the crew had to shout at one another and use sign language. We cleaned out the bilges, and, fortunately, this being new construction, not as much sludge had accumulated, so these weren't half as bad as the bilges I previously tackled in ship repair.

Monday morning saw the crew gathered at the start of the shift, handing our timecards to Carol on the main deck of the AS39. She collected the cards, then informed us we'd split up, with half the crew needle gunning in one of the compartments and the other half working cleanup down on the pier. Lamar and I and a couple other scalers were sent down to the pier.

Carol went back and forth between the two worksites. During one of her trips down the gangway, I heard her holler, "Come on...get this fucking shit off the pier!" Lamar and I were picking up trash. He asked me for a cigarette, and when I stopped, Carol came up behind me. "You'd get a lot more done, Nolan, if you weren't standing there with your thumb up your ass."

Although I practiced on the bus ride, the "get along to go along" college kid in me automatically surfaced, and I froze. My mouth went dry and my heart beat hard against my chest. *Come on*, I told myself. I took a deep breath and summoned the power of Saint Vinny. What would he do if he were standing beside me? His imagined presence provided the inspiration I needed.

I dropped the trash in my hands, looked Carol square in the face, and said, "Yeah...yeah...yeah," plenty loud enough for everyone to hear. Lamar kept his head down, but I could tell he was trying not to laugh, because his shoulders bobbed up and down.

My words did more than take Carol by surprise; they stopped her in her tracks. She stood there, glanced around, wavered a little and blinked, then some color rose in her cheeks and she found her groove. "I told you to get to work, god damn it!"

I didn't budge. Summoning my best Vinny imitation—my features calm, my words loud and clear—I repeated, "Yeah...yeah...yeah."

Carol sputtered, for once at a loss for words. Lamar straightened up and looked at us, his eyes dancing, and Carol pursed her lips and turned around and headed back up the gangway, muttering something unintelligible along the way. I heard snippets of "son of a bitch" and "fucking shit," as she went, but I didn't care.

Lamar's smile split his face in two, and he slapped my hand. "Damn, Nolan...you 'yeah-yeah-yeah'd' her."

Did that just happen? I beamed, disbelieving, and felt a beautiful warmth wash over me. *I did it! Thank you, Saint Vinny.*

I pulled it off, and wanted to jump up and down and cheer, but channeling Vinny's serious demeanor, I managed to play it cool. That's what he would have done.

Esther walked over and patted my shoulder. "Right on, Nolan. I've been waitin' for something like this to happen. You don't have to stand around and take it, like poor ol' Bob does."

We all went back to work cleaning up the pier. After tossing the last of the trash bags in the dumpster, Lamar and Esther and I joined the other scalers on the ship needle gunning. Carol was there, but she didn't say anything to me. She didn't even make eye contact. Did I have Carol Garcia over a barrel? Probably not. *Don't get ahead of yourself, young man...just keep imitating Vinny. Take it one step at a time.*

The crew spent the rest of the shift needle gunning and deck grinding, and as we finished, the Warden happened by. Carol must have complained about me, because Hildebrand took me into the passageway. *Now what?* Was he going to hand me a layoff notice? Fire me?

Taking my arm and leaning in close, the Warden said in a low voice, "Now, you be nice to Carol."

I hesitated for a second then, remembering Vinny, deadpanned, "I'll be as nice to her as she is to me."

Hildebrand pursed his lips. "You just get along with her, Nolan."

With Saint Vinny watching over me, I stood my ground, looked the Warden in the eye, and calmly repeated, "I'll be as nice to her as she is to me."

Hildebrand walked out of the compartment scowling, with his hands jammed into his coverall pockets. The whistle blew, and we were done with our shift.

Riding home on the bus, I kept replaying '*yeah-yeah-yeah*' in my head, each time saying it with a dash more swagger. By the time I reached downtown, I was mentally playing the lead in my own reality TV show. What could have been "Nolan's Last Stand" turned out to be "A Star is Born." I savored my moment of triumph. With a self-satisfied smile on my face, a feeling of empowerment flowed through me. *I don't have to be buffaloed by Carol Garcia,* I told myself. *As a matter of fact, I don't have to be buffaloed by ANYBODY.*

The smile remained in place all the way home. Looking out the bus window, I said under my breath, "I've got that shipyard in the palm of my hand." That evening, to celebrate, I took myself out to dinner at a nice restaurant on Broadway.

I had learned how to go out to dinner as a single person. That sounds strange now, but it was something I had to figure out how to do comfortably. The first time I went out to dinner on my own, I picked a busy, fancy downtown restaurant, and the waiter seated me in the middle of the room. There I was, sitting quietly, all alone, and all I noticed were the couples and groups surrounding me—talking, eating, drinking, having a great time—and the growing line of people by the door, eyeing me while waiting for a table to become available. I lost my appetite.

With a little practice, I figured out how to go to a neighborhood café, somewhere low-key, and ask the waiter for a corner table. I also brought along something to read. I took my time and savored my meal, unhurried. After a couple tries, I ended up enjoying going out for dinner with myself, like tonight.

Back in the shipyard the next day, my burgeoning self-confidence didn't get tested by Carol. It wasn't that her personality changed—she continued to be as profane and mean-spirited as ever—but Carol's venom was directed like buckshot at the entire crew, not at me individually. I collected my holiday pay after Thanksgiving and continued working at Lockheed without another thought of quitting.

Two weeks later, I was surprised to get some overtime work. The white hat in charge of ship scalers on the AS39 was a man named E. I. Cross. The "E" stood for Elmo, which is what my fellow scalers called him, although never to his face. No one assumed first-name familiarity with a hard-ass like E. I. Cross.

A lean, stern, patriarchal figure with a ruddy complexion and square jaw, Elmo wore steel-rimmed glasses and maintained a blustery demeanor. He spoke to Hildebrand about needing two scalers for overtime work coming up Saturday, and Hildebrand passed the word to Carol, who told me to be there by eight. I'm not sure if it was Elmo or Hildebrand who picked me, but I knew the decision wasn't Carol's. *She wasn't riding me anymore*, I thought, *but she sure as hell won't do me any favors either.* I grinned. *I don't care who made the decision; I just want some overtime pay, and I don't mind giving up a Saturday for it.*

That morning found me entering the gate at a quarter to eight. The shipyard was a different place on a Saturday, eerily quiet, almost like a ghost town. It was the first time I noticed the sound of water lapping at the pier.

I was joined in the locker room by another scaler, a guy named Chris Wells. There were a handful of ship scalers my age but, as far as I knew, Chris was the only one who, like me, had a four-year college degree.

Wells had graduated from the University of Washington, where he was a member of the crew team—the coxswain. Small and compact, he had a build something between a flyweight wrestler and a racehorse jockey. Besides being a college athlete, Chris was "Mister Personality," upbeat, energetic, and gregarious. He possessed the sort of good humor that helped make work a little lighter, turning the mundane into fun, or at least making fun of it. I liked him immediately, and we became fast friends.

The whistle blew at eight, just like during the work week, and as Wells finished changing into his coveralls, I descended the worn wooden steps outside the men's locker room. The shipyard appeared more spacious without the chaotic jumble of workers below. Only one lone, imposing figure waited at the bottom of the steps. He had a capital "F" on his hard hat. There were three ship scaler foremen at Lockheed; I had met the Warden and had heard about Washington, who supervised the sandblasters, but I'd never encountered Isaiah Davis, the third foreman.

Davis was a barrel-chested Black man with hardened features, gray-flecked hair, and deep lines across his forehead. He was staring at me, arms folded across his chest, all business. "Are you *NOLAN*?" he bellowed, then, without waiting for an answer, yelled, "GET YOUR ASS DOWN HERE, AND BRING THAT OTHER WHITE BOY WITH YOU!"

Davis's voice echoed off the building like a thunderclap, and I jumped—literally—both feet lifting off the steps. When I landed, I turned around and headed back up the wooden steps, double-time, my heavy boots tapping out an amazingly agile staccato rhythm.

I threw open the door to find Wells sitting beside his locker, lacing his steel-toed boots. My sentences came out in breathless gasps. "There's this angry…this big guy…he's yelling."

Wells cocked his head and squinted at me. "What…?" His hands hovered in midair, tightening his shoelaces.

"Forget it. JUST GET DOWN HERE!" I shouted, wide eyed, motioning with both hands as I backed to the door. "Come on!"

Wells was right behind me, and we danced down the staircase in tandem.

"Gimme your timecards!" was Davis's next command. Grabbing them from us, he jammed the cards into his pocket without a glance, then turned and marched off. "This way," he growled. Wells and I followed like obedient sheep. We strode lockstep across the yard, silently heading to the AS39. Davis had two sets of yellow rain gear tucked under one arm, and his demeanor did not invite conversation. The implicit message was *Do as you're told, and don't go asking any damn fool questions*. I remembered hearing that Davis's nickname was "Chief Black Cloud." I never heard the story behind it but I could see the handle was a perfect fit. Storms lay ahead.

We marched down the pier and up the aluminum gangway to the AS39. Stepping off midship, we followed Davis as he turned aft.

"You two are gonna hose down this passageway and get it ready to be painted," he told us over his shoulder. "Hose it down and blow it dry."

"Shouldn't be too difficult," Wells said under his breath as we exchanged glances.

"Sounds easy," I whispered back.

It wasn't.

Davis took us to the back of the passageway, beside a fire station where a long canvas hose was coiled up. He grabbed the bright red plastic nozzle and turned to look at us. "You hose down the passageway, top to bottom. After you get through, coil the hose back up and sweep the water off the deck. Then you go down the passageway and blow it dry with an air hose. Do this side, then do the starboard side." The three of us stood in silence for a moment, then Davis flung the nozzle onto the deck and walked away.

Wells and I got into our rain gear, pulling the yellow plastic clothing on over our coveralls. The passageway ran almost the entire length of the ship, and the job would have been easy with smooth walls, but there were hundreds of angles and flanges on the bulkhead and overhead that would need to be hosed in and around. The hose was fifty feet long, and we began by running it out on the deck, then doubling it back to where we would start. Wells held the nozzle as I handled the brass valve.

"Ready?" I asked. Wells nodded, and I opened up the valve to full pressure. The three-inch canvas hose, which had been as limp as overcooked spaghetti, suddenly came alive, jolting into a rigid straight line as water flooded it. The nozzle end flew out of Wells's hands and landed on the deck, the hose taut as a length of steel pipe.

"Jesus, this thing is a monster," Wells shouted to me over his shoulder.

We both grabbed for the nozzle, and Wells got his hands on it first. "I got it…I got it."

We stood there for a second with Wells gripping what looked like a solid, thick canvas rod. I braced myself behind him with my hands on the hose. "Okay, Chris, let 'er rip."

Aiming the hose down the passageway, Wells twisted open the red nozzle. A solid line of water shot out in front of us, and when he directed the stream into the overhead, the water ricocheted right back at us, just as forcefully. Wells tried to control the spray into the angles, but the hose seemed to have a life of its own. It took the two of us to control it, with me straddling the hose a few feet behind Wells, who cuffed the end under one arm and controlled the nozzle with both hands.

"Okay, that's better," Wells eventually hollered. Between the roar of gushing water and the spray banging off the steel bulkhead, we had to yell at each other to be understood.

"I need my swimming trunks," Wells called out.

"Yeah," I shouted, "and a snorkel and mask."

We began to get the hang of it, moving slowly, step by step, two guys riding an oversized, unforgiving snake. It was now clear to me why we were doing this on a weekend: anyone working within fifty feet would have been drenched. Like a lot of work in the shipyard, I realized there was a lot more to this job than met the eye, even on a task that seemed simple. It was impossible to hose a bracket or crossbeam without the water deflecting back at us in a shower, running down our hard hats and off our rain gear, but eventually Wells began to get a feel for the hose and angled the spray with a little more finesse.

"Doing this gives me a little more respect for firefighters," I shouted. "This must be what it's like controlling a fire hose."

"Right," he yelled back, "the difference is, when something goes wrong, we end up getting wet. Those guys end up dead."

We kept at it, working as a team, and went as far as the hose would take us. Then we coiled the hose back up and started all over again with a new hose from the next fire station. Washing down the port side took us more than three hours. When we finished hosing, I swept water off the deck with a push broom, and Wells came behind me with an air hose to blow the deck dry.

A couple times I glanced at the pier and saw Chief Black Cloud watching us. We moved faster now that we knew what we were doing, and got started on the starboard side by lunchtime. The whistle blew at twelve, like always, and Wells and I headed back to the empty locker room.

I grabbed my lunch pail from my locker and sat down with Wells at one of the wooden tables, just like a regular workday, except we were all alone. It felt as if we were eating in a library or a museum, somewhere we were supposed to be quiet and keep still, but the strangeness fell away as Wells and I began eating.

"So, how did you end up working here?" I asked.

Chris Wells's story was different from mine. "I first worked at Lockheed while I was a student at the University of Washington. I was part of the men's crew team, and one of the university boosters helped guys like me get part-time work during the off season." Wells took a bite of sandwich. "That's how I got my foot in the door. I joined the union after graduation and got hired on full time."

I knew nothing about the sport of rowing but was impressed with his stories about training on Lake Washington and competing in faraway regattas, on waterways like the Thames or the Nile. Chris still kept busy athletically, working to stay in shape. He wasn't resting on his laurels. Although modest about his accomplishments, I could tell Wells had been "big time" at the UW, making the varsity team.

His future career plans were as amorphous as mine. "For now," he said, "I just want to make some money, get ahead…you know, enjoy what the city has to offer. I'll figure out the rest as I go."

"Me too." I nodded, finally connecting with a kindred spirit in the shipyard, which was satisfying.

After lunch, the afternoon shift involved us hosing the rest of the starboard side. We finished with about an hour to go, and Davis met us on the pier. His features were hard, a black granite statue.

"You finish both sides?"

"Yes, we got it all washed," I said.

"Dried too?"

"Yes, and we drained and rolled the hoses back at each station." I recited my lines like a schoolboy.

I expected him to turn us loose right then, but instead he said, matter-of-factly, "Go on up to the locker room, dry out, and punch the clock at four." That meant, instead of punching out right after we finished, Wells and I would get our full eight hours of overtime. Maybe Chief Black Cloud wasn't such a hard-ass after all.

Wells and I headed to the locker room and stripped off our rain gear. My coveralls were wet, and my boots were soaked, but I didn't care. I was already spending my fat paycheck in my head. After finishing our coffee and punching out at four, we said so long and headed our separate ways, but something told me I hadn't seen the last of Christopher Wells.

CHAPTER 11

Back on the weather deck of the AS39 on Monday morning, I handed Carol my timecard. For the next couple weeks our crew continued the same routine as before, although there seemed to be more general cleanup and less deck grinding.

"That's 'cause this ship is getting ready to be delivered," Lamar told me. "We'll finish building it, make it look pretty, then turn it over to the sailor boys and be outta here."

"Will our crew move over to the AS40?"

"Who knows?" he said with a shrug. "I was looking for a job when I got here, and I'll be looking for a job when I leave."

By now I had internalized that bit of existential philosophy. It served as the psychological buffer against losing your job. You worked hard, you got paid, and when one job was finished, you went on to the next one. The part that nobody said out loud was "And I hope there *will* be a next one." None of us had control over what that "next job" might be, so remaining stoic and philosophical became our mental armor.

Lamar summed it up with "We'll worry about tomorrow, *tomorrow*."

About three weeks after my Saturday overtime, I handed my timecard to Carol, but she didn't take it. "Keep it," she said with a smirk. "Go to the second-deck mike and find Hildebrand."

Now what? Is there still a "next job" for me, or has Carol found a way to get rid of me? Trying to remain cool and look unruffled, I tucked my timecard back into my pocket and headed down to the second deck. As I passed Lamar, he gave me a sideways glance and said softly, "You take care now, Nolan, hear?"

I found the Warden, distracted and animated as always, talking with a couple leadmen. "Just a minute, Nolan," he said in the middle of his conversation, extending his open hand to me. I gave him my timecard and waited. After they wrapped up, Hildebrand turned my way. "Follow me."

We went back up the ladder, then aft to the fantail. A white hat was leaning on the taffrail with his back to us, looking out over Elliott Bay, but I recognized him.

"Here's Nolan." Hildebrand handed my timecard to E. I. Cross, the white hat in charge of ship scalers, and left.

Cross silently examined my card. After what felt like a long time, he said, "Nolan…okay." He tucked my card into his breast pocket and fixed his icy blue eyes on me. "You're a sandblaster?"

The first time somebody asked me that question, I lied. Cross stared at me from behind steel-rimmed glasses, his cool gaze boring through me like a laser. *This time, maybe I should just tell the truth.*

"Ah…I was on a sandblasting crew," I said honestly. Cross didn't respond, but the laser stare demanded I play it straight, so I added, "I was a hose puller for the sandblasters in ship repair."

Cross pivoted back to Elliott Bay, let out his breath, then looked at me again and returned my timecard. "All right…we'll get you going on the oh-one deck. You can start forward on the starboard side."

"Okay," I answered, knowing where the space was but not sure what I would be doing there.

"Wait right here." Cross briskly turned on his heels and walked away. I didn't know what job I was being given, but "wait right here" was a green light for a cigarette break.

Five minutes later, Washington, the ship scaler foreman in charge of sandblasters, showed up. "Are you Nolan?" he said, out of breath.

"That's me."

"Gimme your timecard."

I handed Washington my timecard, which he shoved into his shirt pocket.

"Wait here."

Another cigarette.

Fifteen minutes later, Washington returned with a grizzled ship scaler in tow—a wiry Black gentleman with keen eyes and a body that was all angles and sharp edges.

"This is Nolan," Washington told him. "Get him going on the oh-one deck railing and stanchions. Start forward and work aft."

"Using a piss pot?" the older scaler asked.

"Yup," Washington nodded, then turned and left.

The older scaler and I stood there for a moment, looking at each other. He was trim and wore thick glasses, and I saw more salt than pepper in his hair and mustache. He had a shoestring attached to his belt loop, and on the end of the shoestring was a broken hacksaw blade. Taking off his work gloves, he cleared his throat and extended his hand. "L. T. McQuay."

"Nolan," I responded, shaking his hand. I always identified myself as "Nolan" in the shipyard. With only a few exceptions, like L. T. here, or like Lamar, most people were known by their last name. Maybe it was because Lockheed badges and timecards were printed with a worker's last name, or maybe it was a Navy thing. At any rate, I was certain no one on Carol's crew—including Carol—knew my first name. I guess no one needed to know.

L. T. smiled. "Well…let's get to steppin'…"

We made our way down the gangway and across the yard to the tool room. I could tell L. T. was a Lockheed old-timer, because he acknowledged all the people we walked by. Every time someone crossed our path, they said, "Morning, L. T." His response was always the same: "Fine, and you?"

It seemed L. T. knew everyone in the tool room too. "Morning, Matthew." He nodded to the tool room attendant as I leaned on the counter.

"Hello, L. T. What can we do for you today?"

"This here young man needs a piss pot and a sand gun." Turning to me, he said, "Give him your badge, Nolan."

I handed my Lockheed badge to the tool room clerk, who scanned it and handed it back.

"Anything else?" Matthew asked.

"Yeah…give him a length of hose and a face mask too."

Matthew hoisted the piss pot up on the tool room counter, then flopped a thirty-foot length of rubber air hose down next to it, along with a plastic face shield. Like a lot of things in the shipyard, I'm sure there was a proper name for the "piss pot," but I never learned it. The piss pot was a scaled-down version of a sandblasting pot, designed for small blasting jobs. It looked like a metal five-gallon bucket propped up on four legs. The bucket tapered down to a narrow spout ending in a double valve, one side fitted for an air hose and the other fitted for the sand gun hose.

"That's what we need. Thank you, Matthew." Shouldering the coil of the air hose, L. T. turned to me. "Come on, Nolan, and grab that piss pot."

I put the mask and air gun in the piss pot hopper and followed L. T. back to the AS39. On the oh-one deck, L. T. and I set up our equipment. I found an air manifold and got the hose attached, while L. T. brought up a couple five-gallon buckets filled with sand, which looked as if they weighed at least fifty pounds apiece. Despite his gray hair, L. T. handled the heavy buckets with practiced ease.

"Here you go, Nolan." He dumped half a bucket of sand into the piss pot hopper and examined the deck railing. Standing next to the first stanchion, he pointed to some rust spots. "You're gonna clean these up. Start here, then work your way down the railing and the other stanchions."

By now, I had enough experience with pneumatic tools to figure out how to operate the piss pot and sand gun, and L. T. told me the idea was "to get rid of rust spots and leave the good paint in place."

"You're just blasting the rust, Nolan. You don't wanna blast no paint that's good and make them painters do their work all over again." He chuckled. "I've seen some tired old ships come through ship repair, and they was held together with nothing *but* the paint. No." He smiled. "We're gonna leave good paint where it is."

And that was it. L. T. went back to whatever crew he worked with, leaving me to blast the rust spots off the lengthy steel railing and twenty stanchions. I clamped the plastic shield onto my hard hat, turned on the air pressure at the manifold, and got to work. The rust spots, along with any chipped gray paint, blasted away easily; the bare metal underneath started to sparkle a dull silver as the sand struck it. After fifteen minutes, I took a step back to inspect my work, pronounced the first stanchion and length of railing finished, then moved the piss pot and hose down ten feet and went to work on more rust spots.

Working without Carol Garcia looking over my shoulder felt like stepping into fresh air and sunlight after being stuck in a dark, stuffy closet. I hadn't worked on my own since scavenging cardboard for Old Green Teeth. The rest of the morning passed by easily as I worked my way down the railing, completing fourteen stanchions by lunchtime. Consumed with the work, I had no idea I was being watched the whole time.

Washington showed up just before lunch, looked at the railing, then looked at me. He didn't say anything, so I took his silence for approval. After lunch I was back at it, finishing the starboard side and moving my equipment over to the port side. When L. T. appeared from nowhere with two more buckets of sand, I stopped and raised the safety mask from my hard hat.

"Lookin' up?" L. T. asked with a reassuring smile. I wasn't exactly sure what he meant, but I nodded my head in the affirmative. L. T. glanced down the deck and pointed at some hoses tied farther down on the railing. "I'll take care of those for you," he said, grabbing his hacksaw blade and cutting through the ropes holding the hoses. I looked down so he couldn't see me grinning as I shook my head, realizing that L. T. used that piece of hacksaw blade he kept on a string like most scalers used a pocket clasp knife.

Hours later, I'd almost finished the port side when Washington showed up a few minutes before four o'clock. "Back to Garcia tomorrow," he said. "You can leave the equipment here," he added as he handed me my timecard.

I couldn't read anything from Washington's brusque manner. Was the work okay? Had I screwed things up? The fact that I was leaving the tools here, but wasn't being asked to come back tomorrow, bothered me.

"Whatever…," I said under my breath. The whistle blew, and I headed off the ship.

On my way to the men's locker room, I spotted Lamar and waved to him.

"Nolan—say what?—you missed your girlfriend Carol today!" Lamar's grin was infectious.

"I spent the shift sandblasting. Just with a piss pot, but that still counts as sandblasting, right?"

"Lemme see your timecard." Lamar examined it and pointed to the *SB* stamp initialed by Kelly. "Yes, sir…that means you get a premium for blastin'. You're *the Sandman* now, Nolan."

"No, I must have screwed up, because I didn't get the blasting finished, and I'm supposed to be back with you guys tomorrow."

"What happened? You give 'em that 'yeah, yeah, yeah' shit again or something?" Lamar's grin widened, his eyes dancing.

"No…this time I behaved myself." I started up the steps to the locker room. "I don't get it. I thought I did a good job."

Lamar clapped me on the shoulder. "I'm sure you did, Nolan, but it'll be good to get you back tomorrow. Hell, Carol *needs* someone else to rag on. She was wearing us out today. You know Carol…"

The next morning I was back prepping spaces for painters. I still couldn't figure out what went wrong, and I half expected Washington to come get me to finish the job. I supposed it didn't matter. I had my seniority, so I knew I still had a job until the ship was completed.

"Maybe they was just checking you out," Lamar offered.

"Seriously?" That thought hadn't crossed my mind.

Three days later, as the crew cleaned up trash on the fantail, Washington came walking down the breezeway just before the end of the shift. Lamar, Bob, and I were bent over a pile of trash, stuffing garbage sacks, and we spotted Washington at the same time.

Lamar leaned over to me and whispered, "This can only mean one thing." Washington was, after all, the sandblasting foreman. Then Lamar laughed. "Bob, maybe they gonna give *you* a shot at that piss pot."

"No thanks," Bob said, and kept picking up trash.

As Washington approached, I straightened up and Lamar backed away. "Report to Harris on the AS40 tomorrow morning," the foreman told me. "He'll be on the main deck."

I nodded and Washington left. I didn't know it right then, but my days of working for Carol Garcia were over.

Lamar raised his eyebrows. "Maybe you're gonna be 'Mister Sandman' after all, Nolan."

"Who the hell is Harris?"

"Harris? He's the day-shift leadman for sandblasters." Lamar tossed his garbage bag into the dumpster. "Maybe they *was* checking you out."

I threw my garbage sack into the dumpster and looked off into the distance. "Hmmm…maybe."

Working with a piss pot was minor league, and now I was being called up to the majors, to being an honest-to-god sandblaster. I wanted to rise to the occasion, but I was unsure of myself. "Come on, Little Lammy, you can do it," I told myself. But another voice in my head said, "Be honest. You've seen these guys in action. Don't kid yourself…are you really up to this?"

CHAPTER 12

At this point I had worked in the shipyard for six months, had my own apartment on Capitol Hill, and was exploring the singles scene—or at least *trying* to explore it. In a crowded metropolitan setting, I thought this would be easy, but I found it difficult to meet someone to form a relationship with. I remembered the expression "Alone by myself, alone in a crowd of people" and knew I was living proof.

In my five-story apartment building, neighbors kept to themselves. From time to time I socialized with people from the shipyard, but there were at least a dozen men for every woman at Lockheed, so I wasn't likely to find a date at work anytime soon. Most weekends I made plans with old college friends, but some evenings I found myself on my own, with nothing to do and no one to see. I would sit by myself in my living room, watching TV or reading a book as a terrible loneliness gradually enveloped me. At that point I couldn't concentrate, and I'd lie there on the couch, staring at the TV or book, uncomprehending, as tears began to run down my face. *God, I was lonely.* The situation would have been sad if it wasn't so pathetic.

I hadn't seen my buddy Chris in a while because we hadn't worked any more overtime and, of course, we were on different crews. The only time I would see Chris was when we would run into each other at the gate, punching out at the end of the day. Eventually I crossed paths with him, and Chris suggested we commute together. I jumped at the idea. My new routine began with Chris swinging by Capitol Hill each morning and picking me up in his VW microbus. He kept us on time, and I got to start the workday with much-needed camaraderie.

Beginning the day with Wells was the caffeine in my coffee. His energy level—talkative, consistently up, forever moving forward—was contagious. Wells negotiated downtown traffic with one hand on the wheel and the other holding a battered metal coffee cup. From time to time, he'd put his cup in a holder on the dash and grab a steel spring hand grip exerciser.

"What's that for?" I asked.

"It's for exactly what it *looks like* it's for…I'm in training."

"Training for what?" I grinned. "You exercise that right hand every night as it is." I hadn't quite graduated from my junior high school level of male humor, but Wells was serious. He kept his eyes on the road, pumping away with the grip exerciser.

"As a coxswain, I need to maintain my hand strength for steering the scull."

"You're in training? College is over."

"I'm training for the Olympics."

I laughed, assuming Chris was joking. He set the exerciser aside and drank more coffee. A minute or two passed, and since Chris didn't say anything else, I changed the subject. "Remember the foreman we worked for, Davis?"

"Sure I do. Everyone calls him 'Chief Black Cloud,' and he has a tendency to mix it up with people."

"That's the guy," I said. "I hear lots of stories—some are even believable. And you're right, a few involve him putting up his dukes."

"They tell me he's not shy about picking a fight," Chris said.

"From what I hear," I added, "he has a bad habit of going toe-to-toe with someone who happens to be, you know, the former Golden Gloves of Seattle, and then he gets his ass whipped."

"But he keeps coming back for more," Chris said, shaking his head, "that's what they tell me about Chief Black Cloud."

"You ever hear the one about Davis *shooting* someone?" I asked.

"Sure. I heard after his daughter got married, he shot his son-in-law. But that's a little hard to believe."

"Actually," I said, "I've worked for Davis a few times now. Gotten to know him a little. One afternoon during a cigarette break, we started bullshitting, you know, joking around."

Chris took another sip of coffee and narrowed his eyes. "So you asked him about the shooting?"

"Well, I referred to it, and Davis stopped what he was doing and became indignant. 'That was an accident,' he yelled, 'a goddamn accident. Even the police report said it was an accident.'" I shook my head, then looked at Chris. "I was floored."

"So he *did* shoot his son-in-law," Chris said.

"Sounds like it," I replied. "I let it drop after that. Davis was pissed and, besides, I don't think I really wanted to know the details…" The truth was, this situation was so far out of my range of experience, I wouldn't have known what else to say to the man.

We drove along in silence for a few minutes, then I told Chris about getting assigned to Harris' crew.

"Don't know him," he said.

"Neither do I, but I hear he's the leadman for the sandblasters on day shift. Hopefully, this'll get me blasting full time."

"Well, good luck. You get extra pay for sandblasting. When I see you at the end of the day, you can let me know."

Chris looked for a spot in the parking lot while I reflected on the different people I was encountering at Lockheed. Characters like Lamar, Davis, and L. T. McQuay…I realized I gravitated to these guys. Being connected to them, even casually through work, made me feel like I was in a different league. These people were not simply characters: they were men of depth who got things done and accomplished their work quietly, with ease and good humor. They were strong, capable individuals who reflected complete confidence in themselves. These men had different personalities, but each had a sense of presence I respected. Talking to them, bullshitting with them, and working side by side with them brought out something in me. It generated a feeling of camaraderie, and I told myself that being part of the team meant that I had some of those characteristics too. That's what I *wanted* to believe anyway, and that notion helped define who I was, or who I was trying to be. At any rate, I knew I wanted whatever it was they had.

I punched in, and when the whistle blew, I headed over to the AS40 and up the aluminum gangway with a little more energy in my step, a feeling of expectation. Since I didn't know Harris, I looked for an orange hard hat with an "L" on it.

"Are you Nolan?" a voice sounded behind me. Turning, I saw a medium-built Black man in faded blue coveralls. He had a pointy goatee, and his left eyelid was at half mast, which I think they call a "drooping eye."

"Yeah. Are you Harris?"

"That's right," he said, taking my timecard. "Follow me."

We walked forward to the bow, where a crane had landed a giant sand pot alongside a pallet of sandblasting hose. Four ship scalers were standing around the pot smoking cigarettes. I immediately recognized Richards, the pot tender, who spoke up when our eyes met.

"Back for round two, huh, Nolan?"

"That's what they tell me," I said, trying to sound nonchalant and confident.

The other blasters—Dunbar, Eddie, and Espy—I remembered from ship repair. Harris pointed to Eddie. "He's got your gear."

Eddie handed me a green canvas duffel bag, and as the other guys started to get ready, I pulled out rain gear and a brand-new sandblasting hood. Never having worn one, I wanted to stand there and admire it—I could smell the thick new rubber—but I set it aside and got busy slipping into the rain gear. Then I picked up the hood. I had watched the sandblasters get suited up enough times to have a basic idea of what to do, but having a hood there in my hands for the first time, I realized I wasn't exactly sure how to proceed. The other guys helped me out while I fumbled, turning the hood inside out and trying to figure out how to secure the mask straps.

Dunbar got my air hose hooked up to a manifold while Eddie showed me how to fit a piece of plate glass in the face mask. Spreading the back straps wide with one hand, I cradled the front of the face mask with the other hand and attached the air nozzle. When I locked it in place, a stream of air whistled through the mask.

"You can tone the air down here." Dunbar pointed to a little valve underneath the mask. "Just get a steady stream."

I regulated the air flow down to a reasonable breeze, then Eddie helped me put the face mask on and cinch up the rubber straps at the back of my head.

"That okay?" he asked. "You want it snug but not too tight."

I gave him a thumbs-up, tugged down on the hood skirt to get a good fit, and cinched the skirt belt around my waist.

Okay, I thought, *at least I look like a sandblaster*. The first thing I noticed while wearing the hood was the stream of air blowing into my face: it was noisy but it cooled me off. The second was how restricted my field of vision was, limited by that two-by-four-inch plate of safety glass mounted in the front of my mask. I could only see things directly in front of me. To notice anything left, right, up, or down required swiveling my upper body in that direction.

Between my earplugs and the sound made by the streaming air, I could hear only muffled sound from outside my hood, which was unusual for the shipyard. I was accustomed to a blanket of noise continually ruffling around me. As I moved my head from side to side, getting used to the little glass window, I could see the other guys finish setting up. Espy had his hood folded under his arm and was smoking one last cigarette.

Four sandblasting hoses were attached to the sand pot, and each had a heavy-duty spotlight taped to the end, just short of the steel nozzle. With my gear complete, I picked up one hose and waved to show I was ready.

Espy came up close to me and shouted at the side of my hood, "If you need less sand, bump that trigger twice."

I gave him a thumbs-up.

"And if you want more, you give it three bumps, and Richards will open it up at the pot."

I nodded my understanding and hoped I didn't appear as out of my element as I felt. *I'm pretending to be a goddamned sandblaster, in front of a bunch of* real-life *sandblasters!*

Espy leaned back in. "Okay then. We're doing four sections at a time in this passageway. You be in the back, Nolan, and we'll be ahead of you. We're each gonna blast one section. Start on the deck, then work your way up into the overhead."

I nodded and held my sandblasting hose with both hands as Espy pulled his hood on and made a lasso motion, signaling the other guys to start up. Planks of narrow scaffolding, platforms two feet high, ran down the center of the passageway, allowing us to reach the overhead. Each of the blasters pulled their hoses forward and stood next to their platforms, and I followed suit. We made a line, with Espy in front of me, then Dunbar, and Eddie all the way forward. The plan was for each of us to blast one section, then move on as a group, blasting the next four sections, then the four after that, and so on to the end of the passageway.

Espy fired up his hose, and the rest of us joined in. The passageway instantly became enveloped in a gritty swirling cloud of black sand. I leaned down and blasted around the scaffolding, cleaning up some spots on the deck, then started to work my way up the bulkhead. Careful not to accidentally shoot Espy, I pointed the heavy nozzle up into the I-beams, shining the floodlight on the angles and corners of the overhead steel girders. This was more demanding than blasting the exposed, flat hull of a ship out in the open, as I'd seen in ship repair. With four of us in a relatively confined space, all blasting at the same time, I was in the middle of a dark, violent sandstorm.

I carefully swept through my section, paying attention to rust spots in corners and hard-to-reach angles, then shut off my hose and stepped down from the scaffolding. I figured I finished my section in about forty minutes. As the sand settled and the air cleared, I pulled off my hood, interested to see how the other guys were doing.

No one was there. *What the hell happened?*

I laid my hose on the deck, set my hood to the side, and walked back to the fantail. The three other blasters were all standing by the pot with Richards, huddled together and smoking cigarettes.

"You finished, Nolan?" Espy asked. Clearly, everyone worked a lot faster than I did, knocking out their sections with enough time left over to get their gear off and go back to the sand pot to have a smoke.

"Yeah…guess I gotta take it up a notch, huh?"

No one replied. Everyone just stood there, looking at me and smoking. Eventually, Richards turned to adjust the sand pot, and Espy dropped his cigarette on the deck and crushed it out. "Okay, let's move up a section," he said. The other two blasters followed suit, stamping out their smokes.

We all dragged our scaffolding farther up the passageway and pulled our hoses forward, then lined up in the same order, with me in the back.

"Everybody good to go?" Espy hollered, surveying us. The other men answered by putting their hoods on.

I pulled my hood over my head and cinched up the belt in front. The air whistled across my face, but I could still hear Espy firing up his hose. The muffled sound was followed by a billowing black cloud of sand once again filling the passageway. *Okay*, I told myself, *let's get moving. GET ON THIS.*

My wristwatch was buried underneath elbow-length gloves, rain gear, coveralls, and the sleeve of my work shirt, so I couldn't actually time myself, but I knew I went faster and figured I got my section blasted in about a half hour. However, when the sand settled and I looked around, all the guys were aft again at the fantail by the sand pot, smoking cigarettes.

Christ…I gotta do better.

The crew was talking when I approached, and I thought I overheard something about "Little Elmo," a reference to Elmo Cross, the ship scaler white hat. *Goddamnit…were they talking about me?* Little Elmo was a handle I definitely didn't want to inherit—it implied I was there as Cross's boy and not on my own merits. I pictured Harris showing up at the end of the shift to pull my ass off the sandblasting crew, returning me to Carol Garcia's crew with my tail between my legs.

Eddie offered me a cigarette, took a drag on his, and blew a stream of smoke. "Just give it a light, quick blast, Nolan. Just enough to get it cleaned up."

"No bare metal on this job," Dunbar added. "The paint it ain't. You gotta *leave* the good paint." It was the same advice L. T. McQuay had given me about blasting with the piss pot.

When we finished our cigarette break, everyone dragged their scaffold platforms forward again, then went back for the hoses and air lines. No words were exchanged; these guys had done this a thousand times.

We blasted the next section and I *knew* I was going faster, but all the guys still finished ahead of me. Smoking back at the fantail, no one said anything. We went back to the passageway and moved the scaffolding and our gear forward. Before we fired up though, Eddie said to the other guys, "Hold on a minute," then walked back to my section and got up on my scaffolding. He pointed overhead to the rust spots, tracing his finger along a rusty patch on the I-beam. "Look here, Nolan. You're doing good, but you're doing *too* good. All the painters need is you gettin' rid of this." Eddie touched the rust, then he motioned to the rest of the beam. "You're gonna leave any paint that's good. Just blast the rust. That's all they want us to do. Don't waste your time blasting the whole damn thing, turnin' it all into bare metal. Takes too long." Then he smiled and said in a lower voice, "Just blast what needs blastin'."

"Got it," I said. "Thanks."

Everyone put their hoods on, got into position, and fired up. Vowing to move faster and only go after the rust spots, I kept up a strong pace. Even with the stream of air blowing in my face, sweat rolled off my head. In probably a little less than thirty minutes, I stepped down and took my hood off, but like before, the other guys still finished ahead of me. *Christ almighty!*

With an hour to go before lunch, we had time to move our gear and blast another series of bulkheads.

"You're doing better, Nolan," Eddie said. "You just need more practice to get a little faster."

I nodded in agreement. *What could I say?* It was my first day on the job, I was learning as I was going, and these guys had been sandblasting for years.

On the next section, I still finished last, silently cursing myself.

When we pulled our gear up to the following series of bulkheads, Eddie took me aside again. "How about this? You take my place in the front and blast the first section, and I'll be in the back. You blast as much as you can for about twenty minutes, go fast and light, then shut off, even if you ain't done. When we move up, we'll skip one section. Then when we fire up again, I'll finish off whatever you left and blast the next one too."

Dunbar was listening in and nodded his agreement before I could answer. "Yeah, that'll work. Then we'll all move quicker."

We got into the rearranged order and started pulling on our gear. *Fast and light, fast and light,* I kept telling myself as I secured my hood, then pulled down the blasting skirt and cinched the belt at my waist. Espy gave the signal, and we all fired up. This time I sprinted through the blasting like I was running the hundred-yard dash. My hose was flying, making crazy impressions on the steel, and I made sure not to shoot myself in the process. Although I didn't complete my section, I got a lot of it done within the twenty minutes.

When the sand cleared and I took my hood off, sweat was rolling down my face, neck, shoulders, and arms. Drenched and disappointed, I could see I was still the last to shut down, but this time the other guys didn't have time to get a cigarette back at the fantail. At least I was *closer* to keeping pace. As we got the gear ready to move, my shoulders slumped, and sweat started running out the sleeves of my raincoat. I was taking a beating, but I was still standing in the ring.

"That's good, Nolan," Eddie told me. "That's more like it. You're doing better." It was a good note to break for lunch on. Everyone tore off their rain gear and headed off the ship at the whistle.

The afternoon shift moved quickly, with Eddie blasting his section plus whatever I had left over. I hated myself for being a drag on the crew and especially for creating extra work for Eddie, but at least I was getting faster. Each time we moved up, I had a little less left over for Eddie to blast. By the time we were ready to knock off for the day, I was getting through just about all of my section—not as fast as the other guys, of course, but at least my work was in the ballpark.

When I stripped off my rain gear at the end of the shift, my coveralls were soaked all the way through. I leaned against a stanchion, hunched over and breathing hard, but I couldn't wait to come back and do it all over again. I was determined to keep up with these guys and prove myself.

Harris showed up a few minutes before the whistle blew and handed us our timecards. He didn't say anything, so I assumed he was happy enough with the work. None of the guys mentioned Eddie doing the extra blasting; we just headed toward the gangway.

Crossing the yard on the way to the locker room, I caught up with Eddie, matching his stride. "Hey…thanks for the help today."

"No problem, Nolan."

"Really," I said, stopping for a second, "thanks for helping me out."

Eddie looked at me with a knowing expression. "Just keep at it, Nolan. You'll get it."

"Thanks again," I said.

I met Chris in the parking lot, and as I climbed into the VW, he looked at my coveralls, drenched in perspiration, and chuckled. "You're soaked."

I recounted my shift from start to finish, ending with "But I can make this work. I know I can do it. I can run with these guys."

Always the friend, Chris smiled and clapped me on the shoulder. "You *can* do it." Then he started driving and added, "It's going to happen because you decided to *make it* happen."

Coming from a guy who had steered the University of Washington's crew team to victory, a guy who was training to make the United States Olympic Team, Chris's support and encouragement meant a lot to me.

As he navigated the road, Chris said, "You and I both know being successful means you have to grab the opportunity in front of you, grab it by the lapels, hold on tight, and work it to your advantage." Now he was smiling. "And you don't let go until you get where you want to be. Besides"—he laughed—"the battle that seems impossible *is the only one worth fighting*."

CHAPTER 13

As I walked through the gate the next morning for my *second* day as a sandblaster, anticipation and energy lifted my step. A sense of purpose, of renewed enthusiasm, of *belonging* pumped inside me. *Chris was right*, I thought, *you gotta make things happen for yourself.* Adrenaline would power me through the shift today. It *had* to. Yesterday taught me the crew could only move as fast as its slowest sandblaster, and I was determined to carry my weight, not be the weak link in the chain, not be seen as "Little Elmo."

Making my way forward along the passageway on the AS40, I passed the newly blasted sections, which had a fresh coat of paint from swing shift. The platforms and hoses and other equipment were right where we had left them, and leadman Harris was standing beside it all, ready to take my timecard.

Espy, Dunbar, and Eddie stood down at the fantail, huddled with Richards by the sand pot. Everyone was having one last smoke before getting started. I joined them, standing next to Eddie.

Espy took a long drag from his cigarette. "So, how we wanna line up today?" The question wasn't directed to anyone in particular; he just threw it out there.

I didn't say anything, but Eddie crushed out his cigarette and spoke up. "Nolan's gettin' after it now…let's go back to the regular lineup." Turning to me, he added, "You don't need to skip no spaces today, right, Brother Nols?"

I could have kissed him. "Right." If my level of motivation wasn't high enough already, Eddie's vote of confidence put me over the top.

"Then let's do it!" Eddie exclaimed. Dunbar nodded his agreement, and Espy gave the "fire up" sign to Richards, who went to work pressurizing the hoses.

Working my section, I moved like a sandblasting maniac, *fast-fast-fast*, eyes scanning everywhere to make sure I didn't miss a single rust spot. It wouldn't do me any good to keep up with these guys and not have the space properly blasted. The last thing I wanted was to finish on time and have everyone wait while I went back to re-blast something I'd missed. No way would I let that happen.

I was still the last guy done—of course—but the other blasters didn't finish much ahead of me. We moved all our gear farther up the passageway, having a smoke while our hoods were off, then fired up again after Espy gave the signal. This time around, I finished right after the other guys. Eddie walked back to look over my work, then grinned. "Damn, Nolan, you're getting the motherfucker done!" I was high as a kite.

Dunbar joined in, too, with "Brother Nols, hot as coals." He touched where I had blasted and added a "*tsssss*" sound, as if it burned his finger.

We finished off the starboard-side passageway and began the process of hauling all our gear, platforms included, back to the fantail so we could blast the port side. Making the trips back and forth, I got comments from Eddie and Dunbar like "You're doing good, Nolan" and "Right on, Brother Nols." Even dour Espy seemed pleased.

I was gradually becoming a member of the team. I already respected and felt connected to Richards—he was our elder statesman, our graybeard, and I regarded him as my mentor. His affable, go-with-the-flow manner made me feel at home. The other guys became familiar the more we worked together. Eddie was a singular character, the most outgoing and personable of the crew. When I got to know him better, I found out that, among other things, Eddie had done time at Walla Walla State Penitentiary. His stories about life in prison were fascinating to me, considering my sheltered background.

"I went to prison on narcotics charges," Eddie told me, "and the funny thing was you could get any kind of drug you wanted once you was in prison. Dope, pills, smack, whatever...you had some money, you could score inside. They might sell you a joint skinny as a toothpick, but you could get it."

More important than the stories was Eddie's willingness to always take the time to help me out. He knew I didn't know what the hell I was doing, but he didn't hold that against me.

Espy was the quiet one: tall, thin, and taciturn. Smart and sharp-tongued, Espy observed the world silently through thick square glasses. He didn't say a lot, but when Espy spoke, he was always interesting, always arresting.

Dunbar was our court jester, energetic and ever ready with something funny to say or do. Dunbar's personality provided that drop of oil we all needed when the gears of our work began to freeze up and lock. His humor kept things moving, even when work stood still.

By the end of the shift that day, I was close to holding my own. Naturally, I still couldn't blast as fast or as well as the other guys—how could I?—but I was working hard to keep up. In the days to come I earned a degree of respect from the rest of the crew because of the way I was busting my ass.

Driving home with Chris that afternoon, I gave him a quick recap of the day's events, inflating my skill level a little, as befitted my Irish American storytelling background. Wells was appropriately impressed, but he and I didn't become animated in our conversation until we began talking about women, our most heartfelt topic.

The next couple weeks saw the sandblasting crew working on other passageways and exterior spaces on the AS40, with my blasting skills and comfort level improving a little each day. At one point, Dunbar even said, "Shit, Nolan, a master blaster can't go no faster." I was finding my groove, as well as becoming one of the guys. The other sandblasters all referred to me as "Brother Nols," so I had a place now as the only White blaster among the crew, the leadman, and the foreman. Between occasional stories about Walla Walla, Eddie continued to fill me in on various tricks of the trade, and his coaching helped me develop my technique. I could see that I actually was—slowly—becoming adept at sandblasting.

"I'm not here for my love of shipbuilding" was a refrain I heard from people over and over in the shipyard, typically in exasperation with a particularly meaningless or annoying task. I understood the statement; it served as another mental defense mechanism. I went along with everyone else and said it too, but I had to admit—at least to myself—that the work was growing on me.

Outside of work, Chris and I had discovered three different Capitol Hill restaurants that offered "all you can eat" specials, so we met three times a week, rotating restaurants and stuffing ourselves. One night we found ourselves at a pizza joint, joking about life in the shipyard as Chris was wolfed down a slice with salami and green peppers.

"Have I told you about Davis and peppers?" I asked.

"Nope," Chris managed to say between bites.

"I was working for Davis one day, and he starts telling me how much he likes peppers." I shook my head. "Not this kind," I said, holding up a slice. "I'm talking about *hot* peppers. 'Never found a pepper that was *too* hot,'" I quoted, doing my best Davis imitation. "'It's them little ones, them little Mexican peppers from south of the border. They're the hottest…that's what I like.' Honest to god, that's what he told me."

Chris started laughing.

"So one day I picked up a jar of 'five alarm' peppers at the grocery store," I explained, "I mean those small *extra hot* peppers from Mexico, and I stuck the jar in my coveralls to give to Davis when we were working out on the pier. Davis didn't miss a beat. He unscrewed the lid, jammed his fingers in, and stuffed two handfuls of peppers into his mouth. Then with no expression at all he raised the jar to his lips and drank the remaining liquid. He wiped his mouth with the back of his hand, handed the jar back, nodded and said, 'Pretty good,' and kept right on working."

"Ya gotta love the shipyard," Chris said, smiling.

"I might not love shipbuilding, but this job pays a great wage and allows me to have a place of my own," I told Chris over my sixth slice of pizza. "Sleeping on my sister's living-room couch was getting old. Real old."

"Yeah, now you're living the high life," Chris joked.

"I don't know about the high life, but the little things are nice. My own space, the freedom to come and go whenever I please. Things like that."

"I *love* having my own place," Chris said, and I knew what that meant: the guy was a natural-born charmer, and I'm sure he wasn't alone all the time in his apartment.

Unlike Chris, I was having less than spectacular results in the world of dating. There were two goals on my horizon: I hoped to find a steady date, and I wanted to figure out my career options. Stay in the shipyard? Do something else? It helped that Chris was at a similar place in his life, and we talked about what the future might hold. We agreed that the first step was to simply find a job and make some money. Now that I was employed full time, had a nice apartment and was putting money in the bank, it was time to decide on the next step.

"If you want to get set up for a career, have you considered graduate school?" Chris asked.

I hadn't. I lumped the prospect of grad school in with the last four years of college—my best-kept secret. So far my bachelor's degree hadn't gotten me anywhere, so why would I do more college? But maybe…I should think about it. "I'm not sure what I'll do," I said, "but for now, you can't beat the pay at Lockheed."

"I'll drink to that," Chris said, raising his glass.

On top of the union wage of $13.50 an hour, I received hazard pay for sandblasting. Throw in some overtime here and there, and I ended up with a great wage for a young guy, especially someone without a family to support or a mortgage to pay.

I attended a Christmas party with some former classmates from Gonzaga, friends who were business majors and now worked for big accounting firms. They were starting off at the bottom of the corporate food chain, wearing nice suits to work and projecting the respectable aura of junior accountants. Here I was, a construction worker, making more money than them. The financial advantage felt good, although I never said so out loud, and I didn't have any illusions about the disparity remaining over time. My buddies would out-earn me in a couple years. For now, though, I enjoyed the fat weekly paychecks and tried to get some mileage out of my newfound blue-collar identity.

To be honest, the job identity meant more than the money. I felt a primal satisfaction in working hard and accomplishing a physical task. Was it a reaction to four years of studying in my dorm room and the college library? At the end of a day of sandblasting, I was bone tired and drenched in sweat, but exultant. The gratification of work successfully completed, in the company of men skilled in their craft, fulfilled me in a way I hadn't experienced in college. I was working twice as hard to keep up with these guys, but every time we finished sandblasting, I felt good about myself. I could stand back and silently admire a job well done.

I ran into Esther, from Carol Garcia's crew, one afternoon at the tool room. I had been blasting for a few months by then, and Esther asked me what I thought about the work.

"Yeah," I said, "I like it. I like it a lot."

Esther grinned and elbowed me in the ribs. "They say once you put that hood on, Nolan, you never want to take it off."

"That's right," I agreed.

Honestly, I couldn't say I felt that way about sandblasting exactly, but I nodded and smiled nonetheless. I *did* enjoy the work, despite it being exhausting, but more than that, I felt pride in my ability to do a difficult job. Along with the camaraderie of the other blasters, that was the part I valued the most: I possessed a specialized skill. I was becoming good at a job that was considered dangerous, doing something not everyone could do. With that knowledge came a sense of self. I could look someone in the eye and tell them, "I'm a sandblaster, working in heavy construction." It wasn't what I studied in college, but who the hell cared? The sense of confidence and strength that came from that identity became important to me.

Unfortunately, it didn't work as a pick-up line. I'd get as far as buying someone a drink, and when the conversation turned to what I did for a living, the other person's interest would fizzle out. Lately, I had experienced a lot of "first dates" but nothing more. I resigned myself to thinking, *Some people are early bloomers, others are late bloomers, and after all of them comes me.* Just stick with it, I told myself.

So…I hung in there and kept pitching. Over time I made enough progress to discover it *was* possible to meet someone in a bar and convince them to come home with me: that much I could accomplish. But encounters like that didn't lead to what I really needed, what I was searching for. I wanted more than just sex; I was hungry for a relationship.

At any rate, my Capitol Hill apartment was outfitted, so at least I had a decent place to bring a date home to. And my bank account was growing. When I was a kid, my dad taught me about personal finance and the rudiments of investing in the stock market, going halfsies with me on my first stock purchase, so I decided to stop by the downtown Merrill Lynch office one afternoon after work to set up an account. Unfortunately, the air of confidence I'd entered the building with began to evaporate the moment I stepped into the offices and saw brokers wearing expensive three-piece suits, silk ties, nice shoes, the works. Enter Brother Nols in his construction uniform.

I was directed to a lounge area with a couple overstuffed chairs and a mahogany table, and I immediately felt uncomfortable, afraid my coveralls would get the chair dirty. Glancing around nervously, I thought, *I don't belong here.*

A broker approached, then backed away a half step when he saw me. "This way." He motioned me into his office and looked me over as he shook my hand. I told him I wanted to open an account. "Okay," he said, "so you work here in town?"

"I work at Lockheed Shipyard on Harbor Island," I said, keeping my chin up. "I'm a sandblaster."

The broker's gaze arched over me. "Sandblasting…oh, is that like painting?"

"No, it's like sandblasting," I answered like a real smart-ass, and I felt good again. Fortunately, I held off on "Don't you know anything about the shipyard, Mister Stockbroker?"

My obstreperous attitude was a reaction to the uneasiness with the surroundings, as well as part of my newly developed sense of who I was. Still in the process of figuring out how to handle my "Joe Construction Worker" reinvention, I hadn't read all the way through the owner's manual yet. I didn't know when to wear the attitude or how to calibrate it.

Another example of adjusting to my new identity happened a month later, when the sandblasting crew got moved to Yard One on Harbor Island. We blasted giant steel modules, which represented the early stages of construction of the AS41, the third submarine tender in Lockheed's Navy contract. Chris Wells was still at Yard Two, so our carpooling came to a halt, and I went back to riding the bus.

My bus route after work involved boarding an express that left the Lockheed parking lot for downtown, then transferring to Capitol Hill. Changing busses during the busy rush hour meant the bus always filled up after two or three stops downtown. From that point, people had to stand in the aisle for their ride home. I'd watch the seats fill with men and women in smart-looking business suits as I sat there with my lunchpail on my lap, thinking about the contrast provided by *my* work clothes: filthy coveralls, scuffed-up steel-toed work boots, and a dirty blue hoodie, topped off with my grimy hard hat.

One afternoon, the bus filled up until the only remaining seat was the one next to me, and nobody in their nice "dress for success" work clothes would sit beside me. People's eyes would scan to the open seat, but when they saw me, their gaze shifted to the ceiling, and they grabbed a hand strap. *So people would rather stand up on the bus at the end of their workday—stand on their ride home—than sit down next to me.* I scowled and looked out the window, suddenly hating everyone.

My work clothes *were* dirty, but to be fair, I also probably looked a little intimidating. I had let my lanky hair grow long, just reaching my shoulders, and sported a bushy, untamed beard. Were people just trying to keep their clothes clean, or was my appearance menacing?

Doesn't matter, I told myself. *Don't hold it against them.* I probably felt the same way before I entered the shipyard. An ironic grin played across my face. Back in college, I would have seen construction work as somehow beneath me. I would have felt like there was a layer of social strata separating a university guy from blue-collar labor, sort of a status thing.

Trying to rationalize the situation and not let it get the better of me, I held my gaze out the window, expressionless. *People identify themselves by what they do. The people on this bus probably think like that because they're up-and-coming business types.* Then I smiled to myself. *I work in heavy construction, which means that Brother Nols knows who he is and what he does.* And with a trace of self-satisfaction, I reminded myself I was good at what I did. My blue-collar identity could serve as my armor.

At work the next day I ate lunch with a group of guys that included a rotund, owl-eyed man we called Franko. He was a pipe fitter and our resident philosopher. Franko had just used the "Well, I'm not here for my love of shipbuilding" rejoinder when he became expansive and told me, "Some people are lucky, Nolan. They love their work." Continuing between mouthfuls of baloney sandwich, he said, "They get paid for doing something they like. Work is an end in itself. Then there are *these* poor bastards"—he swept his half-eaten sandwich through the air—"people who work so they can make money. They take that money and use it to do something they like. Work is a means to an end."

Hmmm, that's interesting. Franko had challenged my thinking. *Two opposite takes on work.* I'd never really thought about work like that. I knew some people enjoyed their work, but what about here? Was there value or meaning in shipyard work, or was being a sandblaster just about earning a paycheck? As a kid, I had assumed the adults I looked up to liked their work. In the land of the free and the home of the brave, everyone had the option of saying, "I quit," and leaving a job they didn't enjoy. They could find something else, right? Now that I was in the middle of it all, it occurred to me that work—and life—was more complicated than that; my short time in the shipyard had taught me that much.

Franko sounded astute and I liked what he had to say, but I thought maybe there was an in-between situation, kind of like what I felt, where a person wasn't necessarily thrilled about their work setting but found satisfaction in the job nonetheless. Sandblasting was dirty, dangerous work, but when you wrapped up your eight-hour shift, you had something to show for it. It wasn't as simple as loving it or not loving it; for me, the work *did* have meaning, because sandblasting was demanding, skilled labor and I did it well. That feeling of pride meant more to me than any recognition, probably even more than the paycheck. But I would *prefer* work that I loved to do, *plus the paycheck.* My dad and Franko would have seen eye to eye. Dad had put it this way: "If you can find something you like to do, something you can become good at and people will *pay you for*, then you've got the world by the tail."

My dad told me that in high school but, like a lot of his advice, it wasn't until now that I was beginning to appreciate and apply his insights. At the time, my dad's words sounded straightforward, but now I understood the depth of his observations. He was talking about more than just work—he was referring to the sort of person who was rewarded and reinforced by their work, and the confidence and mental toughness that developed as a result of it, in addition to the paycheck.

Looking around the locker room and seeing construction workers of all ages, I was confident that most of them took pride in their craft but didn't necessarily *like* the work itself. And what about me? Whatever I eventually pursued, I was sure I wanted my work to be an end in itself; I wanted to do something I loved. The shipyard had built me up and given me confidence, providing far more than just a paycheck, but I didn't necessarily see myself here for the long haul. It wasn't that I was above the work—I just couldn't say that sandblasting was the thing I loved; I loved what it did for me, for the person it made me.

In the back of my mind, I couldn't get away from wanting some sort of work that would tie into my college degree. I'd spent four years busting my ass in school, spent a pile of my folks' money in tuition, and now I wanted something to show for it. I wanted a profession. Which made me ask myself, *What work have I done in the past that I loved, and how could I tie it into a career?* My experience was limited to being a dishwasher, a commercial clam digger, and a short-order cook: nothing that I loved. I liked being a student, because I loved learning, but that wasn't a job, was it? I was paying them; the university wasn't paying me. Then I thought about the summer I spent as a YMCA camp counselor. I enjoyed that job—a lot, in fact—and people told me I was good at it. But that was a college kid's summer job…I couldn't exactly make a career out of that, could I?

The whistle blew and everyone wrapped up. As I crossed the yard and made my way back to the AS41, my mind bounced around with thoughts of work, identity, money, career, and the question of what work I would enjoy.

I remembered more conversations with my dad about future plans during my senior year of high school. The next step had been college, which was a given. Everyone told me a university degree would help me get ahead in life. Looking around, I had my doubts. So far, I couldn't think of how my degree helped me do anything, much less get ahead. Instead of being the foundation upon which I was building my career, my bachelor's degree was something I kept to myself. What good was that?

The shipyard wasn't the sort of place where I could reminisce with coworkers about the good ol' college days. If I had, the only rational response would have been "Well then, what the hell are you doing here?" Good question. What *was* I doing here? Earning a living and biding my time, I suppose. Growing up, probably. Figuring out my life.

I didn't see a career path here, but nothing else was clearly calling out to me, either. At least I was making good money after being perpetually broke for four years. That was progress. Now I needed to dig a little deeper and figure out a line of work that would satisfy me, something that would build on my degree, a career that would serve as an end in itself—while hopefully paying a decent wage. Was that asking too much?

In 1978, just before entering the shipyard. Young, confident, and cocky, I didn't know how much I didn't know. *Image from the author's collection.*

Chris Wells was an incredible guy: funny, gregarious, and adventurous, he was also a United States Olympic athlete. We became fast friends. *David Wells collection.*

The USS *Roark*, the Navy frigate on which I had my first sandblasting near-death experience while trying to impress the foreman. *Naval History and Heritage Command, USN 1141100.*

The Todd Pacific Shipyards in 1977. This shipyard is where I became Mike Nolan Ship Scaler. *MOHAI, Vigor Industrial Collection on Todd Shipyards, 2023.36.70.*

The AS39, USS *Emory S. Land*, submarine tender in the Lockheed shipyard, 1977. Working overtime one weekend on the 39, I met Chris Wells, and found a soulmate in the shipyard. *US Navy photo.*

The AS40, USS *Frank Cable*, sister ship to the AS39, sailing in 1979. I became a sandblaster on this ship (without lying). *Naval History and Heritage Command, National Archives photo, USN 1175488.*

The AS41, USS *McKee*, the third submarine tender built for the Navy by Lockheed Shipyard. I sandblasted giant steel modules which were then welded together to form the ship's structure. *US Navy photo.*

The Coast Guard icebreaker *Polar Star*. The *Polar Star* and her sister ship the *Polar Sea* were built by Lockheed Shipbuilding & Construction Company. *US Coast Guard photo.*

The USS *David R. Ray*, the Navy destroyer on which I first worked as a leadman, supervising a crew of ship scalers on swing shift. *US Navy photo.*

The USS *Sacramento*, circa 1983. The Navy's combat support ship where I was once again a leadman, this time nearly killing one of my crew, Wilfred. *US Navy photo.*

CHAPTER 14

Six months passed. I did all sorts of sandblasting, including the time I fell through the crow's nest of the USS *Roark*. "Acrobatic sandblastin'," as Lamar put it. Despite that mishap, when I overheard Washington telling Harris, "The sandblasters will go to ship repair for two days," that included me now. I was one of the guys. Sometimes another blaster or two were added to our crew for bigger jobs, or we took on extra hose pullers, but over time the core crew remained me, Eddie, Espy, and Dunbar, with Richards running the sand pot.

Coming into my own as a sandblaster was satisfying on a lot of levels. There was the identity, as well as the camaraderie of hardworking, blue-collar men whose company at work I enjoyed. *Maybe I should just stay in the shipyard.* That was an option to consider, now that I had a craft. There was also the possibility of moving up within Lockheed, joining management, and becoming a white hat. Even though it felt like an "us versus them" culture, I was sure most of the white hats started off in a union craft. The company posted job openings and training programs on a regular basis. *Maybe I should look into that.*

When I thought about my friends in the city, guys I kept up with from college, it seemed like everyone else was far ahead of me, working their way up a more defined ladder of success toward a career. Craving their sense of direction, I considered further education—which reminded me of the joke "If you don't know what to do, keep being a student." What would it lead to? What did I want to end up doing? What would I *love* to do? I had worked in the shipyard for over a year and knew that if I worked another year and continued to save money, I could pay for grad school. Maybe I could find a program at the University of Washington, like Chris suggested, something that would lead to a specific career. Maybe that was the path I should take.

Like me, Chris was also making plans and moving forward—only more so. He came by my apartment one afternoon for a beer and told me he was still working out, keeping in competitive rowing shape. "Gotta be ready," he said with subtle confidence.

"Are you still shooting for the Olympics?"

"Definitely."

The possibility of becoming a member of the United States Olympic Team sounded like the longest of long shots. "That's hard to even imagine."

"Well…start imagining." Chris smiled. "Annnnnd," he added with a bigger grin, "I've got a date tonight."

"Yeah! Now we're talking. Does this mean you're avoiding nukedom?" *Nukedom* was Chris's term for the absence of a sex life. Again, he just smiled.

If trying out for the Olympics and being busy dating someone weren't enough, Chris was looking for a second job, something at night, on top of working at Lockheed during the day. "Probably a restaurant," he said. "I've worked as a waiter before, and it's a great way to meet the ladies."

I started laughing. Typical Wells.

"What's so funny? Can't you see me as a zesty waiter?"

"Yeah…definitely zesty." That was Chris: eyes wide open to the world, watching for possibilities, moving full speed ahead. I envied his zest.

Monday morning I was back at the shipyard, handing my timecard to Harris aboard the AS41 and having a quick smoke with the other guys.

"Today y'all will be in ship repair," Harris told us. "We got the *Polar Star* in over the weekend. Gonna blast the hull."

The *Polar Star* and the *Polar Sea*, gigantic Coast Guard icebreakers built by Lockheed, returned from the Arctic from time to time for maintenance and repairs. Eddie looked at the mammoth hull as we walked along the dry dock. "It don't get any better than this." Sandblasting a smooth, gargantuan hull, in broad daylight was the easiest type of blasting.

"Broad side of a barn," Dunbar added, "even Washington might be able to hit it."

"Yeah…maybe," Eddie said.

Everyone laughed, but that didn't mean there couldn't be problems. Any sandblasting job involving more than one person was complicated by the fact that one blaster could inadvertently shoot another. That rarely happened with experienced guys like Dunbar and Eddie, but when I got hit—*WOW*—it *hurt*, and I jumped, even returning a little bit of the fire to make sure the other blaster knew where I was and didn't do it again.

The *Polar Star* was perched on wooden blocks on the dry dock, where Richards had four hoses running out from the sand pot. Two more ship scalers showed up to help as hose pullers. Eddie, Dunbar, Espy, and I finished getting our equipment on, grabbed our hoses, and set up underneath the bow. We would blast four abreast, working our way to the ass end with the hose pullers following behind us.

This would be eight hours of easy blasting, I told myself, *if it weren't for that damn trigger.* The trigger—the on/off switch mounted on the sandblasting hose—had to be depressed continually to operate the piston that kept the sand flowing. It was a safety feature known as the "dead man's switch"—*what an uplifting term!* The idea was if a sandblaster had a heart attack and dropped dead on the job, the hose would automatically shut off instead of shooting one of the other blasters or flaying wildly through the air and clobbering somebody. Dunbar claimed it was so that the shipyard didn't have to pay you for any extra blasting after you died. The downside of the dead man's switch was that I found it impossible to hold it down for hours at a time without my hand cramping up or going numb.

Eddie approached me with something in his hand. "Brother Nols, put this in your pocket," He said this quietly, looking around furtively to see if anyone was watching us. He handed me a little wooden wedge attached to a leather shoestring. "When you get blasting, put the string around your wrist and shove the wedge under the trigger. That'll jam it on and keep the hose going, give your hand a rest." Eddie smiled. "If you drop your hose or something, the string will pull the wedge out."

"Got it," I said. "Thanks."

"Just don't let Thompson catch you with it," Eddie added with a wink.

Thompson, the "Safety Man," was a young Black white hat who would write you up for not having your safety glasses on, or for working in a space that wasn't properly ventilated, or for deck grinding without a respirator, or a hundred other safety violations. None of the union guys were "buddies" with white hats, but we co-existed. Not so for Thompson. Everything he did was safety oriented, made sense, and was for our own good—and we hated him for it. I could tell that Thompson knew the score, which must have been a burden for him to carry around at work each day.

Dunbar did a great imitation of Thompson coming home at the end of the day, telling his wife in a high-pitched voice, "*I wrote up three guys for safety violations today, honey, so do we get to have sex tonight?*" Pretty funny.

Sandblasting the hull of the *Polar Star* came off without a hitch, no one got shot, and it was the easiest blasting I'd ever done. The wedge helped too, and Thompson, wherever he was, never caught on.

More difficult sandblasting jobs often involved heights. Sometimes we simply stood on scaffolding or climbed up on a riser and blasted away; other jobs required us to scale several stories of scaffolding, erected one on top of the other, or ascend a series of ship's ladders and blast as we scaled the rungs. Jobs like that excluded Dunbar, who had acrophobia, but even without being phobic, most sandblasters didn't jump at the chance to climb sixty or eighty feet in the air to do their work. For reasons that now defy logic, I enjoyed blasting from heights.

As a kid, I was the one who wanted to climb the tallest tree or get up on the roof. I loved jumping off the high dive at the pool or staring down from a bridge railing. Now at Lockheed—young, fearless, and clearly eager for more sandblasting experience—I was the first guy to volunteer for any special sandblasting situations, towering heights included. *Put me in the game, Coach!*

"I'm just glad," Dunbar confided to me, "it's your ass up there and not mine."

The other reason I didn't shy away from heights was because it made me the "go-to" guy in that particular situation, which fed my hungry ego and need to be accepted. What could be more motivating than being the person the foreman wanted for a demanding job?

Sometimes the difficulty wasn't heights; it was getting your nozzle to the point of contact, simple as that sounds. It's not easy wedging your head into a tight overhead space holding a cumbersome sandblasting hose with a prodigious steel nozzle, especially considering the layers of clothing we had on: our work clothes, covered by coveralls, covered by rain gear, covered by a substantial rubber sandblaster's hood. Besides being buried in layers, we were straining to see our work through a two-by-four-inch plate of safety glass.

"Here, Nolan, try this one," Espy said, handing me a specialized, narrow three-inch nozzle. "This'll make it easier." The short, stubby nozzle was more maneuverable in tight spaces but harder to control, because it lacked the counterbalancing heft of the larger, standard steel nozzle. "This one's handy too." Espy handed me a nozzle formed in a ninety-degree angle. "Good for blasting 'round corners." True, but even harder to control, because I constantly fought the kickback created by the unusual shape.

Over time, I became comfortable using specialized nozzles, but those circumstances were child's play compared to blasting in enclosed spaces.

Blasting inside a constricted, narrow tank was the toughest and scariest sandblasting situation I ever encountered.

Naval ships have lots of tanks, for all different purposes: fuel tanks, diesel oil tanks, freshwater tanks, sewage tanks, ballast tanks…the list goes on. Some tanks are huge. A Navy destroyer's fuel tanks have a volume equivalent to half an Olympic-size swimming pool. Other tanks are constructed to fit around and between equipment within the ship. There is no "excess space" on a sea-going vessel. Tanks can be narrow, long, even serpentine in order to save room. One day I might be blasting with the guys in a tank twice the size of my living room, while the next day I could be blasting in a constricted tank by myself, wriggling along with my belly to the floor, like a snake in a drainpipe.

On board a fast frigate, I was once assigned to blast a tank whose opening wasn't much larger than an industrial air duct. Eddie and I spent the better part of four hours running hoses along ladders and through passageways just to get set up. It wasn't until after lunch that I got my hood on and stood by the tank's entrance.

Harris showed up and looked around the compartment. "You guys all set to go?"

Eddie gazed at the equipment, a cigarette dangling from his lips. He'd been topside to check with Richards, who was running the sand pot from the pier. A lengthy section of ventilation hose hung over the entrance to the tank, and Eddie leaned toward it, watching his cigarette smoke get whisked away. "It's pullin' good," he said. "Yeah, I guess we're ready."

I got down on my hands and knees to crawl into the tank, but Eddie put his hand up. "Hold on there, Brother Nols. You ain't quite ready yet." He rummaged in his duffel bag and found a length of rope, about six feet long. "Here, use this."

"You want me to hang myself first?" I asked.

Eddie smiled. "Put this around your waist a couple times, then tie it off."

"Really?"

"That's right. It's your *in-sur-ance* policy. Sometimes, 'specially in them tight spaces, you get to blasting, and there's so much sand flying 'round that some'll get inside the trigger and jam it. You go to turn it off, and you can't, so the hose keeps blasting. Then what you gonna do?" Eddie laughed. "You can't set it down…damn thing would fly around and beat you to death." He took another drag from his cigarette. "No…you find some angle or pipe or bracket where you can tie the mutherfucker down, then you can get your ass outta there in one piece."

It made perfect sense. I nodded, tying the rope around my waist. "Thanks, Eddie."

I adjusted the air in my hood and made the "lasso" sign, then switched on the floodlight at the end of my hose and got down on all fours. I wriggled into the tank, pulling my hose along with me. It felt as if I were a soldier in combat, down on my belly, holding my rifle and crawling—lizard-like—underneath enemy barbwire.

When I eyed the sides of the tank from the outside, I saw my body would fit, but I didn't take into account how much larger I became with all my sandblasting gear on. I kept bumping the sides. The end of the tank looked to be about seven or eight feet away, illuminated by the light at the end of my hose. Even with a good supply of air whistling inside my hood, sweat slowly began to run from my scalp into my eyes, and I tried to blink it away.

Eddie had suggested I crawl all the way to the end of the tank, then blast as I backed out. But when I crept to what I thought was the end, I saw it wasn't the back of the tank at all; it made a gentle S curve and continued on for another six feet.

I slithered along, pulling my equipment farther in with me, until I reached the actual back of the tank. Rotating my shoulders, I shined my light around and hesitated, trying to decide where to start. *Maybe I should turn around and go out blasting headfirst.* That made sense. I bent at the waist to maneuver my body. My shoulders came up against the sides and top of the tank, and I hunched over and bent harder at the waist, using my legs to push.

I can't turn around. I'M STUCK.

Panic rushed through my core. My body seemed to expand as the sides of the tank closed in on me. I froze. *I'm in a coffin. JESUS FUCKING CHRIST, I'M TRAPPED IN HERE.*

Immobilized, I heard my rapid breathing over the noise of the air line. More sweat ran off my head and into my eyes, and my plate glass started to fog up as I hyperventilated. *Easy, big guy, easy does it.* I tried to talk myself down between big gulps of air. *Relax your body, slow down, straighten out. Come on, take a deep breath... that's better. Focus. Now take another. Okay...better.*

The cool, steady air stream gradually cleared my glass as well as my mind. I stared at the end of the tank, concentrating on where to begin, and cleared my throat as my breathing slowed. *One more deep breath.* I would blast and wiggle out backward, that's all. I could do it "breech birth."

Calm once more, I fired up my hose and started blasting, soon settling into the rhythm of the work. I had to stop once to replace my glass window plate; I always carried a couple extra in my pocket. The first plate became pitted from sand ricocheting off the nearby tank walls, making it hard to see. My flood light got pitted too but, fortunately, never blew out.

I blasted about a foot at a time, starting on the floor and working my way up the sides and overhead. Wiggling backward as I went, I could tell Eddie was taking up slack in the hose and air line. Realizing he was watching out for me helped me remain calm.

Eventually, I sensed a little light coming into the tank, then felt my work boots lip over the edge and my toes touch the deck. I finished off around the entrance, careful to keep my sand spray directed into the tank, then shut off.

As soon as I was done, I stripped my hood off, dropping it onto the deck. I ran a hand through my sweaty hair and lit a cigarette. Eddie was standing in one corner of the compartment, wearing goggles and a respirator. He pulled them off and joined me. "Okay," he said, "no problem, huh?"

"No…no problem," I lied.

"Right on…"

We both sat down and I took a drag on my cigarette. "I blasted that mother bassackwards, and it worked fine. No problem at all."

"Still good to have that rope 'round your waist." Eddie pointed to my middle as he lit up. "Never know when you gonna need *in-sur-ance.*"

"Right," I said, trying to sound cool.

I was drenched in sweat, not to mention exhausted. The two of us sat in silence as the white ghosts rising from our cigarettes bent perpendicular toward the ventilation hose. Harris must have been waiting by the sand pot, because he showed up just a few minutes after I shut down. Crossing in front of us, he looked into the tank and nodded. "Looks good. Y'all finish havin' a break…then get the retrieval equipment set up."

Eddie and I said "Okay" in unison. With an hour to go in the shift, the next part of the job involved getting the sandblasting equipment out of the compartment and running the heavy "retrieval" hose in. Between us and the guys on the next shift, we'd vacuum out the tank and get it ready to be painted. As we sat in the compartment smoking, Eddie looked up. "You did good, Nolan." He flicked the ash from his cigarette and smiled. "Tanks can be a bitch. I ever tell you 'bout the time I was blasting a tank like this and they cut my air off?"

"No," I said, glad to be diverted, "what the hell happened?"

"Well, I was blastin' away, same as you, deep inside a tank. My hose and air line ran up onto the main deck, back to the stern. A crane was loading some equipment on the fantail and set a big fuckin' pallet down right on my air line. And just like that"—Eddie snapped his fingers—"no more air."

We looked at each other and broke up laughing.

"Yeah...me down in that fuckin' tank with the sand flying and no air to breathe."

It felt good to laugh. I didn't say anything to Eddie about my momentary meltdown in the tank. He and I both crushed out our smokes and headed up the ladder to get the retrieval equipment, and we kept busy setting up the retrieval hose until the whistle blew.

After work, sitting by myself on the bus ride home, looking out the window, I could feel the sides of the tank squeeze in on me again, and my chest tightened. The whole episode had lasted less than a minute but seemed interminable at the time. So much for being the "go-to" guy who could handle any sandblasting job. *It's okay,* I reassured myself, *bottom line is, once I calmed myself down, I was fine. I got through it and finished the job, and everything turned out all right.*

I went on to sandblast other small, confined tanks and—thank god—never had a problem in a tight space again. A couple months after that incident, though, I saw firsthand what can happen when there *is* a problem.

Our crew was working on a frigate in ship repair with two extra sandblasters, because we were blasting at two locations on the ship. Richards had six lines running out of the pot, and we divided up into two crews of three blasters each. I was on a crew with Espy and one of the new guys, Rollins. We were blasting a compartment and then a tank—a tight one, just like the problematic one I had faced earlier. When we finished the compartment, Rollins started to organize his gear as if he were going to blast the tank.

Espy spoke up. "Nolan will do the tank. He's—" and that's as far as he got.

Rollins, a small, muscular guy, interrupted. "No, I got it." Grabbing the rest of his gear, he added, "I'm almost ready..."

Espy and I exchanged glances, and he shrugged as if to say, *If Rollins wants to blast it...*We both lit another cigarette.

After Espy and I fitted goggles over our safety glasses and put on respirators, Rollins crawled into the tank. We fed the equipment in behind him, but I was surprised to see he started blasting as soon as he got his body inside, instead of going all the way forward and then blasting his way back out.

I looked at Espy, who was slowly shaking his head but still feeding the sandblast hose and air line in. Rollins had the spray directed away from us, but a cloudy blowback rolled into the compartment anyway, despite the ventilation hoses.

By the movement of the sandblasting hose, I could tell Rollins was working his way farther and farther into the tank, and after forty minutes we stopped feeding the line in to him. I looked at Espy and pulled down my respirator. "He must be at the end of the tank."

"Maybe," Espy said, keeping his eyes on the tank opening. Rollins continued blasting, or at least he kept his hose turned on. I figured the end of the tank must be in pretty bad shape, because Rollins kept blasting for another twenty minutes. At that point I pulled off my respirator. "Do you think he's okay?"

Espy's steady gaze didn't betray any concern or emotion, but then again, he never did. "He ain't shut down his hose or nothing."

"I know." I shook my head. "That's what's got me worried." We were silent for a moment. "Do you think his trigger got jammed? Should we do something? He's been going at it for a while now."

"Yeah…maybe."

I tried to remember if Rollins had tied a piece of rope around his waist, but then it occurred to me there might not be anything to tie his hose down to. Most tanks had pipes, but some had only smooth sides.

After two very long minutes, Espy said, "His trigger could be jammed. He might have to pinch it."

"Pinch it?"

"Right…you always take some rope with you, you know, Nolan, in case you gotta tie your hose down, but if it turns out there ain't no place to tie the motherfucker off and you get stuck, then you gotta pinch it."

"What does that mean?"

"You know…pinch the fucker. You bend the hose back on itself, lean on it or hold it down, kneel on it. You pinch it and block the sand."

"Then what happens?"

"It blows up."

I stared at him to make sure he wasn't kidding.

"When you block the hose with a pinch, it makes the hose blow up." Apparently Espy was serious. "Yeah…I've had to do it a couple times."

"It blows up…where?"

"Well…that's the thing. You hope it don't blow up anywhere close to you," Espy said in his usual impassive tone. "That would be bad. You hope it blows farther down the line, somewhere closer to the pot, somewhere away from you."

"Okay…I'll keep that in mind. Now, what should we do about Rollins?"

"Why don't you go topside and tell Richards to shut him down."

I tossed my respirator on the deck and went up the compartment ladder, making my way to the main deck and back to the fantail. Richards was standing by the pot, monitoring the hoses, and his brow furrowed when I explained the situation. Reaching down, he cut the pressure on Rollins's hose.

I went back to the compartment and found Espy standing over the tank opening, still waiting, now joined by Harris.

"And the line's all the way in there?" Harris asked Espy.

"That's right. We ain't pulled no hose out yet."

"Let's have a look." Harris took a flashlight from his coveralls, got down on his hands and knees, and began edging into the tank. He only got about five feet in, then started backing out. "Well, there's the problem." Sitting down on the deck next to the tank entrance, he motioned the flashlight over his shoulder. "That dumb son of a bitch done buried himself."

Espy and I looked at each other. By starting his blasting at the entrance and crawling in, Rollins made the sand accumulate behind him at the narrowest point of the tank, eventually piling up enough sand to block himself in.

"Come on…" Harris sighed, shaking his head in disbelief. "Help me get him outta there."

Flashlight in hand, Shaw eased back into the tank and wriggled in more than the length of his body. I got in behind him about halfway, angling myself alongside Harris' legs, and Espy crouched by the entrance. The three of us scooped out handfuls of sand "bucket brigade" style, and tossed them on the compartment floor. Harris cussed Rollins the whole time, but the work went pretty fast, with Harris moving forward a few inches every minute or so.

The hiss of Rollins's air hose was still going, so I knew he hadn't suffocated in there. Eventually, Espy pulled the blasting hose out of the tank, which made a little more room. It wasn't long before Harris hollered, "I got him…Espy, get the slack out of his air line."

I wiggled backward out of the tank and pulled off my respirator. The compartment was a mess, sand everywhere.

Harris' legs poked out, followed by his body. "That stupid mutherfucker..."

Right behind him came Rollins, who wiggled out fast and sprang to his feet. Ripping away his hood and air line, he threw his equipment onto the deck.

Espy and Harris took a step back, stunned. Rollins's face was a contorted mask of sweat and snot and tears. His eyes darted everywhere, and in a high-pitched voice that sounded like a scared kid, Rollins shouted, "GOD DAMN...GOD DAMN..." His head and upper body shook, soaked through with sweat, and his chest heaved with forced breathing. He reminded me of something wild trapped in a cage.

Harris put his hands up and shouted, "Calm down, man! Calm the fuck down!"

With uncharacteristic emotion, Espy stepped in front of Rollins and yelled, "Shut up, mutherfucker!"

Rollins went quiet for a second, catching his breath, his wild eyes moving between Espy and Harris. Then he grabbed his hard hat and dashed out of the compartment. Harris hesitated, as if trying to decide what to do, then waved his hands. "Let him go." He stooped to pick up the sandblasting hood. "Just let him go."

All of a sudden, the compartment was silent except for the sound of Rollins's air line whistling in his hood. Absently shutting the air valve, Harris looked away and tossed the hood back down on the deck. Then he walked out.

Espy and I looked at each other. What was there to say? We cleaned up the space in silence. When the whistle blew, we headed off the ship for lunch, but I didn't see Rollins in the locker room, and when we returned to the ship, he wasn't there either.

"Musta clocked out early," Espy said. Harris dropped by partway through the cleanup and confirmed this. I never saw Rollins at Lockheed again.

Two weeks after that incident, I was at home in my apartment watching late-night TV when the intercom buzzed.

Chris's voice came through the speaker: "I saw your light on from the street. Are you still up?"

"Yeah, but my apartment is a mess. Let me meet you out there."

I grabbed a six-pack of beer from the fridge and met Chris at the entrance to the apartment building. It was a still, starry night. "Let's sit out in back, and we'll toast the beginning of your restaurant career."

"As a *zesty* waiter," he reminded me.

A patch of grass ran along a hedge behind the building, and we both sat down by some shrubs. Chris looked up at the stars. I gave him a beer, and he leaned back on his elbows.

"Well…I made it," he said quietly.

"Yeah, your first shift at the restaurant." I clinked my bottle against his. "Congratulations."

"No," he said, "the Olympics. I made the Olympic Team."

"*No way.*"

"I shit you not," Chris replied in the most nonchalant manner.

Incredulous, I sat there with my mouth open, gradually realizing that Chris was serious. "Congratulations," I said again, this time slowly.

Wells did it. He was chosen for the Olympics. Someone I knew actually made it into the Olympics. I looked down at my beer, then back at him. I couldn't believe it. *The goddamn United States Olympic Team!* I wanted to salute a flag. Hell, I wanted to salute Chris. I wanted to cheer, to holler and wake all the neighbors and tell them that my buddy Christopher Wells made the United States Olympic Team. But all I could say was "Congratulations" again.

We were quiet as we drank our beer, and the silence fit perfectly, giving the moment a sense of reverence for Chris' accomplishment.

After a while, Chris described the restaurant he'd started working at—a Tex Mex joint down by the Seattle Center—where he was certain he would encounter an unending stream of beautiful young women. Chris didn't say anything else about the Olympics, humble pie as always. I gave him another beer as he started talking about his new schedule.

"I've actually got a good amount of time between day shift and getting down to the restaurant," he explained. "It shouldn't be a problem, and it's just three days a week. At least to start with. I might do some weekends later. Tips are better then."

In the darkness I could see a small smile of satisfaction as Chris stared up at the stars. I had always respected Chris, but now it was more like admiration. I leaned back and opened another beer, softly saying, "Damn, Chris…

He just nodded, tipped his beer my way, and whispered, "Fuckin' A."

We sat there working on another round until we got cold and the grass became damp. Neither of us knew it, parked by the shrubs after midnight and getting silly drinking beer, but that was as close as Chris Wells would ever come to realizing his dream of competing in the Olympics. And rotten as that bit of human misfortune might have been, it paled in comparison to the ultimate fate that awaited my friend at Lockheed Shipyard.

CHAPTER 15

In May 1980, a sleeping volcano in south-central Washington erupted, spewing ash across the state, primarily to the east. Everyone at Lockheed hoped the billowing gray cloud emanating from Mount St. Helens would find its way north and shut down the shipyard, giving us a day off. Unsympathetic winds continued blowing eastward, however, and we kept working as though nothing had happened.

I was approaching two years in the shipyard and was up on the seniority list, having memorized who was ahead of me and immediately behind me. Newer workers came and went on the list below my name, but when an old-timer retired, everyone went up a notch. People rarely spoke openly about the list, but everyone knew exactly where they stood.

My morning routine began with changing in the men's locker room, an ancient wooden structure with floorboards that creaked under the weight of steel-toed boots. I'd sit in front of my locker, stow my lunch pail and thermos, and sip one more cup of coffee while finishing the morning paper, surrounded by familiar faces and the low murmur of morning conversation. The scent of worn denim coveralls, leather work boots, strong coffee, and cigarette smoke hung in the air.

The routine changed every Friday—payday—when each worker started the day downstairs to pick up their paycheck. Cards and gambling were prohibited in the locker room, but that didn't keep people from wagering. Every Friday morning, a popular way to gamble involved playing five-card stud with your paycheck serial number. A group of guys would agree ahead of time to pool ten or twenty dollars each and, upon picking up their checks, compare the six-digit number printed in the corner. Since each check was unique, the serial number became your very own poker hand. You could choose five digits out of the six to make a pair, three of a kind, a full house, and so on. Some guys wagered more, with a few going so far as to bet their entire weekly check.

Once paychecks were distributed, the whistle blew, and everyone drained the last of their coffee, slammed lockers, and shuffled down the stairs to begin the workday. Hundreds of workers crisscrossed the yard in all directions—new construction, ship repair, one of the shops—and began eight hours of labor.

And labor we did. The majority of people I encountered worked hard every day and took pride in their efforts. It was part of the blue-collar identity, the defining characteristic of heavy construction culture. Nobody wanted to be the person seen as "dogging it" or not pitching in to get the job done. Of course, occasional characters proved to be the exception. One such person was called "Sal."

I met Sal when I was with Carol's crew on the AS39. He was a near-sighted, middle-aged guy with a protruding belly and a ruddy complexion, pock-marked and splotched with acne scars. I already knew Sal's reputation when I met him, but I got to see him in action—if you can call it that—cleaning rust from a metal staircase one day.

I passed Sal on my way to the tool room, and he was sitting on the deck staring at the back of the steps—called a ladder—apparently contemplating cleaning them with a wire brush. I returned about fifteen minutes later.

Brush…brush…brush. Sal had begun.

My next trip topside was about an hour after that. Sal had worked up two or three steps.

Brush…brush…brush.

Two hours later, I went up to use the Sani-Can. Sal was taking a cigarette break, wire brush in hand. The rest of the crew could be working circles around Sal, and he would patiently explain, "I only have one gear. I don't go any faster. I just have one speed." *That's for sure.*

Brush…brush…brush.

Since Sal was high on the seniority list, no one could touch him, and Lockheed couldn't fire him unless he got in a fight, slept on the job, or showed up drunk.

The fourth time I passed by Sal was after lunch, on my way to the tool room again. Sal was brushing the steps in the middle of the ladder now. On my return trip, carrying an armful of needle guns, I noticed he'd worked his way to the point of having to raise his hands to eye level in order to do the work. *That'll never last*, I thought. *Too much effort.*

I was right. When I saw him again later in the afternoon, he was still working behind the upper steps, but instead of standing on a stepladder, he had suspended a bosun's chair from an overhead beam. It hung there under the ladder, so he could sit, swaying in midair while brushing the steps in his own little world. A satisfied smile hovered on Sal's face.

Brush…brush…brush.

No doubt Sal would be there until the end of the shift. The steps might even get cleaned in the process.

The typical worker at Lockheed and Todd was not like Sal. Generally, people took far too much pride in their work ethic to ever perform as Sal did; most probably despised him. Since this was heavy construction, people like Sal rarely showed up in the first place. The rest of us kept our heads down, worked hard for eight hours, and tried to avoid characters like Sal—except at lunchtime. The half hour spent sitting in the locker room eating lunch was actually a lot more fun with someone like Sal at the table, a natural-born bullshitter who was probably lying but could spin a good story.

Just like in the high school cafeteria, most people sat at the same table every day, with the same group of guys. If you were new, it was important to figure out what sort of group you were getting yourself into when you decided where to sit.

Some guys spent their entire lunch bitching about their in-laws, or the kitchen pipes that needed repairing, or a show they had watched on TV the night before. The topic would change each day, but the bitching remained the same. These people were easy to identify and important to avoid. Another character to keep away from was the guy who discussed work the entire time—this behavior was known as "building another ship at lunch time."

I've since learned these personality types are universal, found in white-collar as well as blue-collar lunchrooms. Lockheed had its share. Fortunately, there were others—people with something to say, individuals who caused me to think—who made lunch an actual break from work.

One day at my usual lunch table I met someone new: a Filipino American scaler who had been working in Yard One and got transferred to Yard Two. He sat down across from me, so I said, "Hi. I'm Mike Nolan."

"Jimmy Garcia," he said with a smile.

I almost choked on my sandwich.

"Yeah," he said, reading my expression, "Carol Garcia is my mother. Do you know her? Ever work on her crew?"

Still in shock, I gave Jimmy the edited version of my experience working for Carol, leaving out the Styrofoam tubes and the "yeah-yeah-yeahs."

"Oh, she wasn't always like that." Jimmy laughed, seeing the disbelief on my face. "She was a good mom. Really. You gotta understand the situation.

My mother was one of the first women to work here. Look around," Jimmy waved his hand through the air, "This is a rough place. She had to develop a thick skin to fit in. If you're gonna work with sailors, you gotta cuss like a sailor."

I had never considered how Carol got to be the way she was. Or *why* she got that way.

"So she became someone else?"

"Sort of." Jimmy shrugged. "That's how she survived, and that's how she raised me as a single mom."

In the weeks to come I would get to know Jimmy. I liked him, and my understanding of Carol began to change. For one thing, I had never thought of Carol as a mother, nor had I pondered what sort of road Carol had traveled. Viewed with today's sensibilities, Carol would be considered a groundbreaker, a feminist who took on the gender roles of her day.

Looking back, I felt a little guilty in my lack of humanity in judging Carol. She put on her own "identity armor," just as I did. Would things have turned out differently if I'd met Carol later, when I had more experience, rather than when I was new, green, and easily intimidated? Who knows… maybe we would have seen eye to eye. Perhaps I would have understood—and maybe even appreciated—her.

In addition to the various lunchtime conversations and personalities, the one other constant at noon was the sound of dominos being played at the corner table. Every day the same group of gray-haired Black men would huddle at a table around a tan leather mat rolled out for a game, their voices hollering, "Two like that!" as a domino chip, or "bone," was slammed down on the leather mat.

"Make it six!"

"Four mo', don't-cha-know!"

Just like gambling with paychecks, I never saw money change hands, but judging from the enthusiasm of the players, I'm sure somebody's take-home pay was being won or lost.

When the whistle blew, everyone would wrap up and head back to work for the afternoon shift. By now I understood the work ship scalers did and how long it typically took to get a particular job done. Every assignment was organized in Lockheed's "top-down" management structure, with the communication flowing in one direction, from the white hats to the foreman to the leadman and finally to the crew, with very little conversation floating back upstream. Feedback was never invited.

I recall being on the dry dock with the sandblasting crew, looking at the underside of an ocean-going barge we were setting up to blast. Kelly stood under the bow, talking to Harris about how he wanted it done: "Set up two hoses to run the length of the barge, with two guys blasting and two pulling hose. Start over there, on the starboard side, and get this son of a bitch knocked out today, 'cause it'll get painted on swing and towed out tomorrow morning, at the tide."

"I'll have 'em blast down the starboard side, swing 'round the ass end, and come up the port side," Harris repeated back.

Standing a few feet away, we all looked at each other and thought the same thing: *Ain't gonna happen*. The underside of the barge was covered in rust; it would take a little more than one shift to do a decent job. We had more than two hoses, though, and could easily get the job done in time if we ran four lines and Kelly brought over a couple hose pullers from new construction.

"What do you think?" I asked Eddie, who was shaking his head.

"Not enough time." He glanced at Espy, who looked doubtful. "You wanna talk to him?"

Espy looked at the barge, nodded his head, and said, "Okay," but his eyes told me his heart wasn't in it. He walked over to where Washington and Harris stood on the pier. "For this job, if you want my opinion—" and that was as far as he got.

"Opinions are like assholes," Washington lectured while shifting his belly. "Everyone's got one, and they all stink. Now get to work." End of conversation.

Espy, Eddie, Dunbar, and I got busy getting the equipment in place. We blasted the barge with two hoses, working down the starboard side and up the port side. Even though we worked hard right up until the end of the shift, we didn't finish the job. About forty feet remained under the port bow to blast. Didn't matter. The painters painted it anyway, rust and all, and the barge sailed with the early morning tide. I would have liked to finish that job properly, but maybe it wasn't important to the white hat. Maybe it wasn't important to the barge owners. I'll never know. What I *did* know was that no one was interested in hearing from the assholes at the bottom of the pyramid.

At least upper management communicated with one another. Through the white hats, sandblasters were coordinated with painters, who were coordinated with riggers, and so on. The result was one craft didn't tend to get in the way of another. Communication between the white hats was crucial for keeping the work moving and preventing one craft from standing around. That's how Lockheed made money in ship repair: getting work completed quickly and efficiently. Miscommunication on the management level was rare, and I witnessed it only once.

I was on a sandblasting job with Dunbar, and we got our instructions directly from the white hat, E. I. Cross. Elmo usually went through channels when communicating work assignments, but this time he bypassed the foreman and leadman because he was in a hurry.

Dunbar and I stood on the dry dock underneath a ship, next to a square steel plate removed from its hull. The plate was the size of a car, cut out from the ship's supporting ribs to allow riggers to load machinery into the engine room. When Dunbar and I looked into the open space, we saw two welders at work.

"I think what we got goin'," Dunbar explained, "is we're gonna blast the space they opened up with that square down there." He pointed to the steel plate, then said, "After they're done welding, we'll blast the compartment and hop down and blast the steel plate, then it'll get welded back into the hull." Dunbar motioned with his hands—one palm representing the steel plate, the other the side of the ship—and slapped them together. "After that, we'll blast the outside."

Sounds easy enough, I thought.

"You wanna do the blastin', Brother Nols?" Dunbar asked with a smile. He knew I did.

"Sure thing." I went to gather my equipment and saw Elmo walking down the pier.

He hurried over to the dry dock, and his eyes widened. "You guys haven't started yet?"

I pointed into the space. "There are a couple welders in there working."

"Start blasting anyway."

Surprised, I looked at Dunbar, who was getting the hose in place. He shrugged his shoulders and let Richards know we were ready to go, while I held my hood under one arm and peered up into the compartment, ready to blast the moment the welders finished. Arcs of golden sparks showered down the ship's hull from where the two were working. One of the guys glanced over at me, and I hollered, "We need to start blasting here."

He turned back to his work and kept welding. Neither one acknowledged me.

I raised an eyebrow at Dunbar. "What do we do?"

He shrugged. "Keep waitin', I guess."

I knew Elmo would have a fit if he came back again and found us standing here, but I waited—impatiently—with my hood in my hands. Time seemed to slow down, then eventually stop altogether. I pictured the eruption of Mount St. Elmo, with me and Dunbar being engulfed in the lava.

Finally, I set my hood down. "I can't stand it anymore. Elmo Cross is going to wander back down here and blow a gasket when he sees us waiting around."

"Well, what you wanna do, Nolan?" Dunbar took a long drag from his cigarette and leaned up against the bulkhead, much more relaxed than me. "Nothin' we *can* do. They're still workin' in there. There's two of 'em welding. We gotta wait."

My anxiety got the better of me. "No…I'm going to find Elmo and see what he wants us to do."

"It's your funeral."

I stowed my blasting equipment, stepped away from the compartment, and went looking for Elmo Cross.

The smoldering volcano was in the ship repair office at the end of the pier. His steel-gray eyes bore down on me the moment I walked in. "Why aren't you blasting?"

I only got as far as "There are still two welders—"

The blue-gray eyes turned to ice. "YOU TURN ON THAT HOSE, AND IF ANYONE QUESTIONS YOU, TELL THEM *E. I. CROSS* TOLD YOU TO START BLASTING." His face had turned crimson, and a vein pulsed in his neck.

"Even if the welders—"

"*JUST START BLASTING.*"

I made an immediate about-face and marched, double time, down the pier to the dry dock. Dunbar was leaning up against a stack of wooden blocks when he looked up and started laughing. "Elmo say somethin'?" he deadpanned. Cigarette smoke curled out from his nostrils.

"Fire up," was all I said as I hurriedly strapped my hood on. Grabbing the hose with one hand, I climbed into the compartment and, looking back at Dunbar, raised the other in the "let's go" signal. The two welders glanced up but still didn't budge. I pushed the trigger down and let 'er rip.

What happened next was both spectacular and frightening. As my sand spray ricocheted throughout the compartment, two figures flew into the air, jumping between the frames and falling out onto the dry dock, their welding chaps and jackets flapping like wings and their hard hats bouncing along behind them. A confusing tumult of toolboxes, hoses, and welding rods shot upward as though momentarily weightless, each finding its own trajectory. I only witnessed the scene for a moment before the billowing black cloud enveloped the compartment.

Afterward, Dunbar and I cleaned out the sand to prepare the space for the painters. The whole time I kept looking over my shoulder, expecting an enraged welder to come back and threaten me with a blowtorch. Nothing happened. Dunbar and I finished the job and left.

"I guess that's one way to get 'em outta there." Dunbar's smile widened as we walked away from the dry dock. "You're the one who wants the sandblasting experience, Brother Nols. Now you can tell 'em you done blasted welders!"

I just kept walking, still expecting to get cussed out, or maybe hit over the head with a fistful of welding rods.

I recounted the situation to Chris Wells that weekend while we were having coffee. "If there is any justice in this world, E. I. Cross suffered a prolonged ass-chewing from the white hat in charge of welding."

"If there *is* any justice in this world," Chris countered, "the Huskies will take the trophy at today's regatta." It was opening day of the boating season, and Chris was decked out in his school colors: a purple blazer, light tan slacks, and a gold tie. He was getting ready to join other UW Crew alums at the Montlake Cut, hoping to cheer the Huskies on to victory.

"Aye, aye, Commodore Wells," I said, snapping a salute.

As I sat there with Chris over coffee, the world felt right. I was living in the moment, even wishing I could freeze it, like they do in cryogenics, and bring it all back to life at some future time when I was down and needed some good luck. In fact, a time would come when I would remember this scene and try to unfreeze it in my head—with Chris standing there at the top of his game, full of enthusiasm and energy and good humor. Full of life. But I wouldn't be able to bring the scene back, and trying to do so would only make me sad.

CHAPTER 16

During the next three months, a succession of vessels came through ship repair that Eddie, Dunbar, Espy, and I sandblasted. As always, the work was physically demanding, but it never brought us down. The guys talked and joked and knew how to keep things light. Just like everybody else, I repeated the line "I'm not here for my love of shipbuilding," but I had to admit that if I wasn't crazy about shipbuilding, I loved my blue-collar identity and the new attitude and self-confidence that came with it. I felt like I stood taller; I liked being "Brother Nols."

On top of that internal growth, I changed physically. Sandblasting gave me a daily workout, and I was in the best shape of my life, eating like a horse and burning off the calories. When we weren't blasting, we were hauling equipment or shoveling sand—after you blast with it, you have to get rid of it.

Common practice was for sandblasters to shovel the spent sand—piles of it—into Elliott Bay. I never stopped to consider the environmental impact of dumping a small mountain of sand into the waters bordering downtown Seattle. Like a good soldier, I was "only following orders." The sand didn't merit a second thought; putting it back into the waters of Puget Sound wasn't polluting. What difference would that make? It was sand. We were returning the egg to the chicken.

Turns out it wasn't that simple. The sand we used for sandblasting was not real sand. The first time I looked at the dark, coarse material we used for blasting, I figured it came from volcanic beaches around Hawaii. It was jet black and extremely porous, like tiny crystals of lava rock, and was much more abrasive than the light brown sand associated with the golden beaches of Southern California, bare feet, and volleyball.

"It's slag," Espy explained to me, "like welding slag. This isn't sand, Nolan. It's fucking *grit*, and it comes from the steelmaking process."

"Lockheed buys it from a foundry," Eddie joined in. "It's some kinda waste byproduct. Got all sorts of nasty shit in it."

"True grit." Dunbar laughed.

"Yeah, but it's poisonous," continued Espy. "I've heard it's got arsenic in it. But the shit is gritty, so it does the job. Just don't eat any of it, Nolan." That got all three of them laughing. Were they pulling my leg?

I didn't know what was in it, but I recall standing by a hopper of newly delivered sandblast grit one hot afternoon, with the sun beating down on it. My eyes started to water, and I got a sour taste in the back of my throat. Maybe it *did* have something unhealthy in it. The shipyard ended up getting rid of that particular hopper of sand.

Partway through my five years in the shipyard, Lockheed reached a turning point in environmental concerns. The sandblasters were told to change how we got rid of sand. President Nixon formed the Environmental Protection Agency in 1970, so I guess it took only ten years for the news to reach the shipyard. Sandblasters went from shoveling spent sand into the Duwamish Waterway to piling it up and hauling it out. God knows where the sand was taken from there, but we didn't toss it into the water anymore.

The next challenge was to contain sand during the sandblasting process itself. This presented a particular problem in ship repair, where we tended to blast a ship's outer surface on the dry dock, which was wide open on either end. Riggers suspended a mammoth tarpaulin from wing wall to wing wall, all the way down to the deck, like a towering shower curtain. When we sandblasted behind that tarp, the spray made it bulge out like the nose of the Goodyear Blimp, but it did the job; most of the grit fell to the dry dock's deck. From there, we shoveled it into low-slung hoppers, which were emptied by cranes into dump trucks. Besides the poisonous stuff already in the grit, spent sand contained whatever we blasted off the side of the ship: rust, steel, and copper-based marine paint.

Obviously, the shipyard was a dirty, dangerous place to work. There are more deaths annually in construction than in any other field in America. I could see potential hazards surrounding me; I didn't need Thompson, the safety man, crawling around the yard telling me to wear my hard hat and put on my safety glasses. I don't remember exactly *worrying* about the dangers, because I was young and invincible: accidents would happen, but they would happen to someone else, not me. But, every now and then, a fatality would occur that would push those dangers—at least momentarily—to the front of my mind.

"You know a scaler on the AS39, a White guy named Bob?" Espy asked me one afternoon.

"Sure I do. I worked with a guy named Bob on Carol Garcia's crew. Nice guy."

"That's him," Espy said with his usual flat affect. "He died yesterday."

"No shit…what happened?"

"The guy fell in a tank." Espy stared at me with impassive eyes.

"I heard about that," Dunbar said. "It happened in that big ol' tanker tied up at the pier."

"Yeah, people been talkin' about that." Eddie nodded. "His crew was cleaning a diesel tank, and he fell going down into it."

I had seen that tanker: a giant diesel fuel ship from Alaska. That would mean Bob fell in a tank the size of a basketball court, at least thirty feet down to the steel deck.

"There's a two-foot gap between the hatch and the ladder in the tank," Espy continued. "He fell lowering himself down to the ladder, trying to get his foot on a rung."

"It'd be easy to do," Dunbar said. "Diesel fuel is slippery. The tank and ladder would be covered in it. Going in to clean that shit, the man probably had rubber boots and rubber gloves on. Real easy to slip."

"He splattered on the deck," Espy said. "Washington tried to give him mouth-to-mouth, but the mutherfucker was already dead."

I stood there listening to it all, my emotions gradually catching up to what I was hearing. "That's a goddamn shame. I knew Bob. I worked with him. He was a nice guy."

"He's a dead guy now," Espy said.

"That's part of workin' here," Eddie added, "just like any heavy construction. It'd be the same in a foundry or a big factory. It's a dangerous place to work. There's accidents. People die."

Nobody said anything else as we went back to work. I got busy with other things and the shift progressed, but Bob's death stayed on my mind. A little part of me suddenly felt desperate to get the hell out of the shipyard. I needed to leave—alive—and figure out what to do with the rest of my life.

Visiting home that weekend, I felt something new in how I was treated. Nothing was said out loud—maybe it was just the way I carried myself these days—but I sensed there was respect for the work I was doing, or for who I had become. Something beyond sandblasting skills had been acquired.

"I've been thinking about what's down the road for me," I told my dad.

"Beyond the shipyard?"

"Yeah…ships come and go. Right now the work is good, the pay is terrific, but I don't think it's a good long-term plan, unless I go into management. The old-timers tell me it's the nature of shipbuilding. The industry is up and down. Right now it's up, but…" I made a diving motion with my hand.

"Try something else," Dad said. "Why not?"

"What if I change jobs but don't make the same wage?"

"So what?" Dad shrugged. "If it leads to doing something you love, it'll be worth the difference in pay. Probably more. Besides, being successful, or being happy for that matter, is more than just about the money."

"I like what I'm doing," I said, but then I backed up. "Actually, I like what sandblasting has done for me, what it's taught me about myself. I owe the shipyard a lot for that. But I can't stay there. I'm on the upward curve of the work cycle right now, but eventually it'll come back down."

"This was something completely new for you," Dad said, "and you made it work. You figured it out. That tells me you can probably do whatever you want. You can take that much and run with it."

"Yeah…that's the part I'm still trying to figure out. Where to run."

I wasn't sure what the next step was, but my thinking had shifted from work I thought I *ought* to do, to work I knew I *wanted* to do. "This'll sound funny, but remember that summer I worked as a YMCA camp counselor? I really liked that job, working with kids, helping them out. Maybe I could do some work like that."

"Why not?" Dad said again. "Give it a try. If it doesn't work, quit and go do something else. Or go back to the shipyard." We were quiet for a second, then Dad patted my shoulder and added, "Besides, the most important thing is who you are, not what you do, and you've got the 'who you are' part figured out now."

"Thanks, Dad."

That was one of the great things about my father: support was always there. And it helped, because figuring out my career direction had been bearing down on me, flooding the back of my mind. Maybe all I needed to do was give myself permission to pursue whatever I felt like doing. Like Dad said, I was the only person I needed to please with my decision.

Yeah, I thought, *why not?* The prospect of working with young people—guiding them, supporting them—felt incredibly appealing. I loved being a camp counselor: the interaction, the guidance, the *fun*. It was a natural fit, and I got rave reviews. I just never connected work at a summer camp to an honest-to-god career.

After all my effort to reinvent myself within the blue-collar world of heavy construction, my college degree might actually come in handy, as a bridge to graduate school. A visit to the UW campus made me think seriously about that path. Of course, I still had tremendous respect for the guys who made a career of construction work, and I was proud of what I could do as a sandblaster. If I didn't stay, I knew that pride would at least be the foundation to build my next move upon. I'd be pursuing something completely different, but maybe a little part of the shipyard would remain with me, hopefully keeping me confident and propelling me forward.

In the meantime, I kept sandblasting and tried not to dwell on people falling to their deaths in tanks, or sandblasting with poisonous sand. But the truth was that personal health hazards and the environmental damage from sandblasting were very real. In 1995, Harbor Island, where Lockheed Shipyard had operated, would be declared an EPA Superfund cleanup site. Different sections of Harbor Island would be decontaminated and restored over time, costing millions of taxpayer dollars. The cleanup of the Lockheed property began in 2018, with the stated goal of "removing polluted soil and seabed, contaminated from paint, metal scrapings, and sandblast grit" that had all been released directly into Elliott Bay. I felt guilty knowing I had contributed to that pollution, *but I had only been following orders.*

CHAPTER 17

Sometime in June, Chris and I were having dinner at one of our "all you can eat" restaurants. I told him I had decided to leave the shipyard and attend graduate school at the University of Washington.

"I can hold my own as a sandblaster," I told Chris, "but I can't stay there. It's not the right place for me. Shipyard work is never going to be something I can say I love doing."

"Graduate school will be your ticket out?"

"That's what I'm thinking…"

"I'll drink to that," he said, raising his glass. "Here's to a fellow Husky!"

"Can you believe it? I visited the campus, met with the admissions people, and checked out the counseling programs. To pursue a career as a therapist, I'd need a PhD in clinical psychology, but that would take me four years. Instead, I found a two-year program in educational psychology, and I'll come out of it with a master's degree in school counseling."

"Sounds good," Chris said. "You worked as a camp counselor once, didn't you?"

"Yes, and I loved it. Of course, I'll have to get accepted into grad school first, but I met with a professor who encouraged me to apply. He thought I would be a good candidate for the program." I laughed. "Incredible…my bachelor of science degree will finally come in handy."

Chris raised his glass again. "Good luck."

"I've done the paperwork, taken the tests, and sent in my application."

"So this is what comes after Lockheed?"

"Like I said, I've got to get in first. But the shipyard got me this far, and surviving there has taught me I can do whatever I want."

"You can," Chris answered.

"There are two factors drawing me to the program. It will lead me directly to a career, and I'd end up working with people one-on-one, helping and guiding them, which is appealing."

"And that's the difference from your biology degree, right? Too general?" Chris asked.

I nodded. "Right. I'll know where I'm going. I'm ready to bleed purple and gold, just like you." We clinked our glasses and started laughing.

On a Saturday late in July, I spent the morning fixing up my apartment and preparing a meal. I had invited my sister Nancy over for lunch. Looking over the apartment, I thought back to sleeping on her couch. Now I felt like I had it together. *Like a regular goddamn adult.*

Before Nancy arrived, I checked the mail, tossing the junk and stopping when I came to an official-looking envelope. The return address was *University of Washington School of Education.* I ripped it open and read, "We are pleased to inform you that you have been accepted…"

My whole body relaxed as I took a deep breath. The door to graduate school was open to me, an invitation that would lead to a career. And it seemed like a line of work that fit perfectly into my dad's job paradigm: something I liked, something I could get good at, and something someone was willing to pay me to do. Dad's voice rang in my ears: *You'll have the world by the tail.* I finally felt some forward momentum.

Nancy arrived, and I showed her the letter. "Check this out."

"You're going to graduate school?"

"That's right. It's a two-year program, and I'll end up working as a school counselor."

Nancy, always supportive of her little brother, put her arm around me. "Why not? I could see you as a counselor. You'd be good at that."

"It means I'll go back to being a full-time student. I've saved enough money to quit the shipyard. I'll leave at the end of August."

"You're probably ready for a change." Nancy put the letter down and looked at me. "It sounds like you've been searching for your next move."

"I've been searching for a while," I told her. I knew graduate school would be something new for me, but I also knew it wouldn't change the person I'd become. "I used to be Mike Nolan College Student, then I became Mike Nolan Construction Worker," I explained to Nancy. "Now, it isn't so much that I'll be Mike Nolan School Counselor…I'm satisfied just being Mike Nolan. That's enough…whatever lies ahead."

"Amen to that," Nancy said.

"Philosophically, I'd always thought 'you are what you do.' Now I think identity runs a little deeper than that. What you do is *part* of who you are—of course it is—but when I think about the other men on the sandblasting crew, I think of them as much more than simply construction workers or sandblasters. Identity *does* run deeper than that. Anyway, I'm sure I'll bring a little of that 'construction worker' ethic with me whatever I take on."

After Nancy left, thoughts of identity kept replaying in my mind. I'd be moving to a white-collar job, while wearing a blue collar underneath. "Can do" optimism convinced me I could take on whatever life threw at me.

I had one more month of work. I'd miss the men on the sandblasting crew, and the weekly paycheck, but the university had things to offer me in return, opening a world of career possibilities, as well as the opportunity to meet someone new and—another optimistic thought—maybe start a relationship.

My sandblasting career would end aboard the USS *David R. Ray*, a Navy destroyer in ship repair undergoing a major overhaul. Sandblasting in the company of Eddie, Dunbar, and Espy would be a fitting way to wrap things up. I'd give my two weeks' notice to Hildebrand, not Washington. I never felt comfortable around that fat bastard, and going through the Warden would complete the circle for me in the shipyard.

Working in ship repair, I hadn't crossed paths with Hildebrand for a few months, but one afternoon in mid-August, I took the long way back from lunch, making my way to the AS39. When I stepped on the main deck, the ship took me by surprise. The AS39 wasn't a vessel under construction anymore; it was a different ship now, a nearly-completed submarine tender, ready to be turned over to the Navy and inhabited by two thousand sailors.

Hildebrand was at his usual perch by the second-deck mike. He looked exactly the same: fidgety body, faded blue coveralls, "F" on his scuffed orange hard hat. The Warden was deep in conversation with two leadmen as I approached. Having rehearsed "I'm here to give two weeks' notice," I also had my backup line, "I was looking for a job when I got here, and I'll be looking for a job when I leave." Turns out I didn't get to say either.

The moment Hildebrand saw me, he broke off from the two leadmen, gently pushing them to the side. "Nolan—good—I want to talk to you." He sounded as though he was expecting me. Before I could say anything, he had me by the arm and was leading me down the passageway.

"Now, look," he began, "I'm putting together a crew on swing shift for the *Ray*."

"I'm already working on the *Ray*."

"I know that, but I want you there on swing. I've talked to Kelly about it."

I skipped the two weeks' notice speech. I hadn't even considered going back to swing. Maybe I should. If I could keep working for a couple more weeks until grad school classes took over my life, I'd put a little more money in the bank. Money for tuition. "Let me think about it."

"Great." Hildebrand slapped me on the back. "You think about it and let me know."

I walked back to ship repair, mulling over the idea. The move to swing meant I wouldn't be sandblasting anymore; I'd go back to being a regular ship scaler. That's why Hildebrand was setting up the crew, not Washington.

Aboard the *Ray*, I talked things over with Eddie. "They want to move me to swing," I told him, "as a scaler."

"Yeah…I wondered if they was doin' a swing shift. I noticed Hildebrand over here talking with Washington the other day, and figured they were up to somethin'."

I also explained that I wanted to go to graduate school.

"More schoolin'?" Eddie grinned. "Why the hell not? Ain't no reason for you to stay here."

I explained that graduate school would move me on to a career, to doing something I loved.

"Hell yeah…this is just a paycheck," Eddie agreed. "Wish I had me a career. Anything would be better than *this* bullshit." We both laughed, but part of me wished I could bring Eddie along with me.

"And you know," Eddie went on, "swing is pretty mellow, 'specially in ship repair. Hell, you're a young guy, Nolan, you got a lot of energy. Maybe you can work nights and do your schoolin' during the day. Do both."

"Why not?" I answered with shipyard confidence. I didn't know if I could hold down work *and* school, but if I couldn't—so what?—I'd quit. There was nothing to lose.

I went to see Hildebrand the next day. "I'm in," I told him.

"Good. Swing shift on the *Ray*," Hildebrand said evenly. "You'll start next week. The white hat on swing is Jacobs. Report to him at four o'clock on Monday."

"Four o'clock on Monday," I repeated. "Got it."

That gave me less than a week to make the transition, but when I thought about it, there wasn't a lot I needed to do. I was changing my working hours, that's all, and a couple weeks after that, I'd begin classes. The big question was who I'd end up with for a leadman. I wondered if, by chance, they'd move Carol Garcia to swing. I smiled at the thought. *I'd do fine with Carol now…I might actually get along with her.*

I told Chris about my situation that weekend. "The only problem to solve is transportation. I have the bus line figured out between my apartment and the University District, but if I move to swing shift, there isn't a bus running at midnight to get me back home from the shipyard."

Chris had his VW bus, relying on it even more now that he was splitting his time between the shipyard and the restaurant job. Like him, I needed a car.

"You definitely need some wheels," Chris said. Then he pivoted. "I'm sitting in with the band tonight after I finish my waiter shift," he said. The restaurant he worked at had live music. "Playing spoons."

"What else would a waiter be playing?" I laughed.

"Seriously," Chris continued, "one of the guys in the band taught me how. I've been working on it, and I'm getting pretty good. You should come down some weekend and catch the show."

I just smiled. "Maybe after I find a car. I'll have my hands full just doing that for now."

The next day I dove into my search. My auto-bargaining experience was limited to my second-hand high school purchase of a 1960 Ford Galaxie 500, pointy tail fins and all. I decided to go whole hog and buy a new car. Why not? I had the money. And this time around I wasn't buying anything with fins on it.

I treated myself to a sports car, a Mazda RX-7, which was a thing of beauty and a joy to drive. I was set. Monday afternoon I pulled up to the main gate in my new car and punched in a little before four o'clock. After changing in the locker room, I made my way to the ship's office aboard the *Ray*. The shift whistle blew on the way in, and I felt out of place not joining the day-shift horde leaving. When the crowd was down to a handful of white hats huddled around a desk, one of them looked up and asked, "Are you Nolan?"

"Yes," I said, wondering where the rest of the crew was.

"I'm Jacobs. Go ahead and sit down." He was a young guy with an easygoing manner, curly dark hair, and thick glasses. Jacobs motioned me to a chair and handed me a sticker with a capital "L" on it. "Here, put this on." The genuine surprise on my face must have shown, because before I could say, "Really?" he added, "Yeah…I want you to be the ship scaler leadman."

"No kidding…" was all I could come up with.

"No, I'm not kidding. E. I. Cross said you'd be up to it. I want you to be the scaler lead for a crew of five here on the *Ray*."

"Ah…okay." My eyebrows rose as I peeled the "L" from the adhesive sticker and placed it on my hard hat, aware I probably looked like the youngest leadman in the shipyard.

Jacobs chuckled as if he'd read my thoughts. "Don't worry, it looks good on you. Arrive a little before four each day, and meet me here in the office. I'll go over this with you." He handed me a legal-sized paper with two carbon copies attached. "This is the day-shift work order, and it details the different jobs we want your crew to complete on swing shift."

There were six tasks written on the form, with spaces between each one where I was supposed to fill in something. "You explain how far you got with every job by the end of the shift," Jacobs said, "and the next morning the day-shift guys know where to begin."

I took it all in, paying close attention to the details while trying to get my head around having my own crew. *I can do this, right? Mike Nolan, college kid, supervising a group of individuals who are probably all older than me, and have more experience than me.* I nodded my head and silently reassured myself. *I've been a scaler for two years now. I know what I'm doing.* Besides, I was educated at the "What Not to Do as a Leadman" school, taught by Professor Carol Garcia. As a matter of fact, I was her star pupil.

"You'll sign these at the end of each shift." Jacobs held up a stack of timecards. "Stamp them for any premium, any additional pay, and then initial each stamp."

"Got it," I said, looking at the cards. I was familiar with timecards and premiums, like the extra pay I received as a sandblaster, but had never filled out or signed one of these myself.

"Of course," Jacobs continued, "as leadman you get any premium your crew members get, since you supervise their work."

"Of course," I answered confidently, though the words "your crew" still sounded strange. Jacobs reviewed more paperwork, then he suggested I walk through the ship to familiarize myself with all the spaces.

The USS *David R. Ray* was a destroyer built in Pascagoula, Mississippi, in the late 1970s. She was over five hundred feet long and carried a crew of more than three hundred. With the day-shift work order in hand, I took myself on a tour, examining each compartment described in the work order and checking out spaces in between. I was struck by how much quieter it was than on day shift. There were just four leadmen during swing, supervising painters, scalers, welders, and machinists, and Jacobs was the only white hat. Other individual workers came and went as needed—electricians, shipwrights, boilermakers—but they were on loan from the AS39 or the AS40.

After I finished my tour from stem to stern—a different, though not unpleasant, way to complete my first shift—Jacobs gave me a list of names and said I would meet my crew tomorrow.

The next day found me standing on the main deck by the gangway, work order in hand, awaiting five ship scalers. I'd already memorized their names and was anxious to attach faces. The first person to show up was Ollie, a sweet, older Black woman with a limp. Next was a middle-aged Black man named Russell, followed by a tall, muscular White guy with long brown hair and an unruly beard, David. On his heels was Harriet, a heavyset, scowling Black woman. Last up was Allen, a thin White guy with red hair who was in his late twenties. Allen was here courtesy of a prison work-release program.

I took each person's timecard as they stepped off the gangway. *So this is how we start.* My entire crew was older than me, and everyone except Allen was an experienced ship scaler. I rationalized *this should make it easy to get things going.*

I started giving out tasks. "Harriet, you'll be on fire watch in the boiler room." The assignment was greeted with a sour expression, but I didn't take it personally. I soon learned that everything Harriet said or did was accompanied by a sour expression. "Ollie, I need you and Russell to wipe down the oh-three passageway and get it ready to be painted. You'll find a couple ladders and a bale of rags at the forward end of the passageway."

"Okay." Ollie nodded. "Come on, Russell." And off they went. It was that easy.

The job assignments went like clockwork, but underneath it all I felt a little intimidated, awaiting a reaction like "Who the hell do you think you are, telling *me* what to do?" Thankfully, it wasn't like that at all. The crew's experience made my job easy; I just needed to assign the task and let them do it. "David, you'll be on fire watch in the engine room," I said. That left Allen as the only crew member I needed to explain anything to.

David went to the fantail to get his fire extinguisher, and by this time Harriet had retrieved hers and was heading to the boiler room. Most people would either cradle the extinguisher in both arms or throw it over their shoulder. Not Harriet. She grabbed the nozzle and dragged the tank by the hose, scraping it along the steel deck behind her and banging it against every hatch she stepped over. Why didn't she just pick the damn thing up and carry it? I didn't ask; I simply checked the task off the work order and kept going.

"Allen, come with me. I'm going to have you sweep down the fantail and clean up back there." We passed David on the way; he was carrying his fire extinguisher under one arm, and he tipped his hard hat in a little salute. I had a broom and dustpan waiting for Allen on the fantail. "Have at it."

That was it. Everyone was on a job. I read through the work order one more time, then folded it up and walked to the bow to have a smoke. The early evening pastel sky reflected softly on Elliott Bay, and I stared at the Seattle skyline while my mind wandered. Each of the little lights twinkling in the early evening across the city represented a person, and I was still on my own, hoping—wanting—to be in a relationship. *There's someone out there for me*, I reassured myself.

An hour later I went to check on everyone. They were all working, doing what they were supposed to do, so I returned to the bow and had another cigarette. The stars were coming out now in the twilight sky, and I reflected on the first rule I'd learned in supervising people: explain the job, make sure they have what they need, then get out of their way. This was, I realized, the quality I appreciated most in the leadmen I'd worked with, people like Harris, who respected and trusted the sandblasters' skills.

After everyone came back from lunch, I toured the ship again, checking on my crew. *My crew*. I shook my head and smiled. Ollie and Russell finished prepping the passageway, and I put them on the next job, cleaning up an oil spill in the engine room. Allen was ready for a new task too, and I continued checking jobs off the work order.

Back in the ship's office, I found Jacobs sitting at his desk going through paperwork. "Everything's clicking along," I told him. "No problem."

"Good...so how do you like swing shift?"

"It's great, and a lot quieter."

"Yeah," he agreed, "not so crazy. Not as much bullshit." He leaned back in his chair and placed his feet on the desk. "Just get through your work order each day, and you'll have it made. As long as your crew is getting the work done, there are only three ways things can blow up on you."

I was pretty sure I knew the three explosions, but I said, "You mean like if one of my guys sinks the ship?"

Jacobs laughed. "Yeah, more or less." He leaned closer to me and cleared his throat. "There are three grounds for termination."

"Right..." I knew the conditions people were fired for but never thought I'd be involved in the firing process.

"First"—Jacobs raised one finger—"if someone is drunk at work. Automatic termination."

"Does that happen very often?"

"Happened last week on day shift. To a ship scaler too."

I hadn't heard about that. "What happened?"

"Older guy named Joe something."

"Joe…," I repeated, thinking about a scaler I knew on day shift. "Older White guy on the AS39?"

"That's him." Jacobs frowned. "Too bad, really. His granddaughter graduated high school and got accepted to college. First one in the family to do it. Joe was celebrating."

"And he got fired?"

"Well, they found him in the locker room, three sheets to the wind with an empty pint of vodka in his coveralls."

"Why didn't they just take him home and let him sleep it off?"

"Doesn't work that way. Rules, you know? Automatic termination."

I thought about Joe; he wasn't someone who would normally show up drunk. That was a one-time thing. There *were* guys who regularly smoked weed in the shipyard or sneaked booze from their locker, and some of them probably deserved to be fired, but not Joe.

I shifted gears. "The second one is fighting, right?"

"That's right." Jacobs nodded. "Automatic termination."

"Hopefully that doesn't happen as often."

"The third one is sleeping on the job," Jacobs said. "They're fired on the spot for that one too."

I stood. "Time for me to check on my crew. Maybe someone will be drunk, get in a fight, and be knocked out cold. With all three conditions met, it'll be a breeze for you to fire them."

"Actually"—Jacobs raised his eyebrows—"the leadman carries out the termination."

"Really?"

"Sorry…company rules. I make the determination and do the paperwork, and you inform the person they're being fired. Then you walk them to their locker, watch them clean it out, and escort them to the gate."

"Isn't that a little over the top?"

"Well, it's so they don't get angry and break something, you know, destroy Lockheed property. Or steal something on their way out." Jacobs shrugged. "You're their direct supervisor, so you have to make sure the termination is done correctly."

"Something to look forward to."

I walked out of the office and went searching for my crew. In the boiler room, Harriet sat parked, unmoving, next to her fire extinguisher. She wore dark glasses, so I couldn't tell if she was watching the welder or sitting there unconscious. Didn't matter. The guy welding wasn't on fire, and neither was the ship. I kept going. One by one, I checked on everybody. They were all working; no one was drunk, rowdy, or asleep, except maybe Harriet. I went back to the bow to have one last smoke.

Standing on the bow, I leaned against the gunwale and gazed out over Elliott Bay. "Talk about a low-key job," I said to no one. "Plenty of cigarette breaks too. If it keeps going like this, I'll get lung cancer in no time."

The shift wound down uneventfully. I completed my notes on the work order and left it for the day-shift supervisor, then filled out and signed the timecards. Jacobs was still at his desk, busy with paperwork. "This crew seems pretty good," I told him. "Maybe I won't have to fire anybody. Damn shame about Joe, though."

Jacobs looked up. "Company rules."

The crew gathered by the gangway just before the whistle blew, and I handed out timecards. *Not bad*, I thought, watching the scalers file down the gangway. My first shift as a leadman, and no "automatic terminations." Nancy was right. *I can make this work.* I patted myself on the back—prematurely. My education in supervising a crew was only beginning.

CHAPTER 18

Over the next few weeks, I settled into my routine of student by day, leadman by night, and surprised myself by being able to handle the demands of both worlds. Wells was on day shift aboard the AS40, so I only saw him on weekends, and even those visits were becoming less frequent because the "zesty waiter" kept busy then, too. We got together one Saturday night after Chris had worked a dinner shift, meeting at his favorite Chinese restaurant, Tai Tung. "Good food, lots of it," Chris told me, "and they're still open when I get off work."

We sat down at an unadorned Formica table. Tai Tung might have a storied history as one of Seattle's oldest Chinese restaurants, but the place wasn't much for decoration, other than an autographed picture of Bruce Lee on the wall. Chris was right about the food, though. We dug into our chop suey.

"So, how do you like UW?" Chris asked, his alumni pride evident.

"It's great." I nodded. "Grad school is different from college. Students are older, a little more mature, and most of them are working, like me."

"You'll love the campus," Chris said. "Have you been down to the boathouse?"

I had to smile. "I've got my hands full getting to school on time and not being late to work, so the only part of campus I've seen is Miller Hall, the building my classes are in. Last week I showed up in my coveralls and hard hat, but I made it to class on time."

Chris laughed. "Must have fit right in."

I was on the run, but Chris kept even busier: full time at Lockheed, the restaurant job on the weekends, training for the Olympics. "And," Chris added, "my girlfriend just moved in with me." There was a lot to like about being Christopher Wells.

Neither of us said it, but one of the things we shared that night at dinner was a sense of acquired direction. We'd both come to the shipyard as an in-between place in our lives, somewhere to make money while we figured out our next move. Now we were moving forward, making something happen, giving shape to our futures.

"How's work on the *Ray*?" Chris asked.

"Good; I like being a leadman, I've got a terrific crew, and the white hat is an easygoing guy."

"There's only one?"

"Yeah, on swing, at least. A guy named Jacobs, and there are four leadmen on board."

"You haven't had to fire anybody?" Chris asked with a grin.

"Actually, someone on day shift did it for me, about a week ago."

Chris hovered above a bowl of chow mein. "What happened?"

"A woman on my crew named Harriet got in a fight in the women's locker room. It happened just before swing shift started, so the day-shift leadman fired Harriet and her sparring partner."

"Automatic termination," Chris said, eating again.

"I didn't have to deal with it. I showed up to work that day, and she was no longer on the crew, which was fine by me. I'm also making a little more money. There's the shift differential for swing—"

"*And* leadman's pay," Chris added.

"Right, lead pay, and I also get any premium someone on my crew gets, because I'm supervising them."

"No shit?"

"Literally." I laughed. "Did you know there's a premium for cleaning up human waste? Two scalers on my crew got it a couple weeks ago when they had to hose out a sewage tank, so I got the pay too, without getting my hands dirty."

"Please," Chris winced in mock revulsion, "not while I'm eating."

I smiled and sipped my tea, realizing how much I missed my buddy Chris these days.

We closed the place that night, eating chow mein, chop suey, and fried rice. Tai Tung became a favorite late-night hangout for me. Being back on swing, my internal clock was resetting to a "late-night" lifestyle, which involved going out after work to get something to eat and unwind. Dick's Hamburger Drive-In was open until the bars closed at two in the morning, and the Doghouse Restaurant, on Aurora Avenue, was open twenty-four hours a day. The welcome sign read "All roads lead to the Doghouse," over a painting of the restaurant with a number of roads leading to it, individually labeled "blondes," "brunettes," and "redheads." It was 1950s humor, and the place served 1950s food, like fried pork chops, and liver and onions.

Back on the *Ray* Monday evening, I had a smoke out on the bow and reflected on what I was learning—not just at graduate school but at the Shipyard School of Management. Some responsibility and a little bit of power came with being a leadman, and it was already clear to me that the best way to exert any power was with the lightest possible touch. When I treated people with dignity, they almost always responded in a dignified manner.

After I finished my cigarette, I went below to the boiler room to check on Ollie and Russell, but found only Ollie cleaning the diamond plate deck. "Where's Russell?"

"It's his time," Ollie said.

I hesitated for a moment. "His time?"

Ollie stopped what she was doing and looked at me. "You serious, Nolan?" When I didn't answer, she explained, "Russell is an old man, so he's got his 'time.' You know, *his time to go*. So that's what he's doin'."

Instead of asking more questions, I said, "Okay, sure…" and walked away.

Later that evening when I saw Russell coming back from the men's locker room, I figured it out. Some older men had "their time," the thirty or forty minutes they went to the john every night. For some guys, this was a nightly ritual you could set your watch by.

I went back to the locker room myself one night to check it out—not while Russell was in there, of course. Instead, I asked David to come with me to get some cleaning supplies from the tool room, and before we headed back to the ship, we made a trip up to my locker so I could get some cigarettes. On our way, we passed the showers and the entrance to the toilets.

"Not much privacy there." I nodded toward the space. The bathroom consisted of a dozen white porcelain toilets all in a row against a back wall, with a little side partition between each one and nothing in front. Anyone walking by could look in and see who was sitting on the john.

"Lockheed don't want us to have privacy," David said. "Management don't want people hanging out in the shitter any longer than they have to. That's why there's no doors."

"Guess these weren't built with discretion in mind."

David, an imposing guy to begin with, scowled and said, "They pay us to work, not to shit."

"Yeah, but when you've got to go, you've got to go." The toilets were unoccupied as we passed by, although I noticed some newspapers on the floor.

David caught my glance. "You get caught reading the newspaper during work hours, you'll get fired. But they still read the paper in there." Now he was grinning.

"How's that?"

"You can shit in there with the sports page on the floor, but you can't be caught *holding* the paper."

"I don't get it."

"To read the paper," he explained, "you just lean forward and read it off the floor."

"You're kidding..."

"Nope. I've seen people do it," David said matter-of-factly. "Wait 'til you see guys turn the pages using their steel-toe work boots. It's impressive. And they never actually touch the paper with their hands."

The next couple months aboard the *Ray* were uneventful as I settled into my schedule. The biggest adjustment was becoming someone who stayed up until midnight, slept to midmorning, then dashed off to classes. After work I began recognizing fellow night owls, the regular customers at the all-night diners. We constituted a zombie subculture within the city.

Although I developed a routine, working in ship repair meant the writing was on the wall: the repairs, maintenance, and upgrades on the *Ray* would eventually be completed, and the ship would return to active duty. My crew would be laid off or transferred. I could deal with either of those scenarios—different from having to fire somebody.

One night Russell found me in the ship's office, where I was filling out timecards. "Nolan, there's a problem."

"What's wrong?"

"I think you better come see."

I followed Russell down a few decks and along a passageway. He stopped outside the magazine storage area, where the ship's ammunition was usually kept. I had sent Allen down there to prep the area for painting.

"In there." Russell nodded toward the space.

I walked into the compartment and almost stepped on Allen, who lay sprawled on the deck beside a puddle of vomit. Russell came in behind me. "No, he ain't dead. Just drunk."

I knelt next to Allen and lifted his head up.

"Damn, it's nasty in here." Russell wrinkled his nose. Next to Allen's feet were his hard hat and an empty bottle of peach schnapps. "Au-to-ma-tic ter-min-a-tion," Russell intoned.

"Maybe," I said, "if Allen were an asshole. But Allen isn't an asshole, is he?"

Russell shook his head. "No."

"So no one is getting fired tonight."

Allen's eyes were shut tight. "Allen," I said, patting his cheek, "Allen, wake up." I turned to Russell. "Help me with him, will ya?" We rolled Allen onto his side.

He wasn't out cold, because his eyelids slowly rose to half mast, and he managed to say, "I'm sick."

"Russell," I said, "let's see if we can get him walking. If he can walk, maybe we can get him over to the locker room."

"Sure. Come on, Allen." Russell took an arm and threw it over his shoulder. As we hoisted Allen up, Russell looked at me. "Nolan...you're all right. 'Specially for a leadman."

Allen struggled to his feet, repeating, "I'm sick," while Russell and I walked him to the main deck, then down the gangway. We were lucky enough to avoid bumping into Jacobs. The only person we saw on the way to the locker room was a welder walking down the pier. "He's sick," I said, nodding toward Allen as we passed.

The long wooden staircase to the men's locker room presented a challenge, but stumbling up the steps helped Allen sober up a little. Russell and I sat him down on a bench beside the lockers, but he waved his arm toward the toilets and mumbled, "No, get me in there."

We juggled Allen into the john, where he wavered in front of a toilet and then started stripping off his coveralls. Next came his trousers and finally his shorts, with everything accumulating around his ankles. Turning around, he sat down heavily on the toilet, at which point Russell asked me, "Do I need to be here for this?"

"No," I answered. "Why don't you go back to the ship and make sure nothing else goes wrong."

As Russell left, Allen shat violently, and I started asking myself, *Do I need to be here for this?* Unfortunately, the answer was yes.

Allen raised his head and groaned as I patted him on the shoulder. "Do what you need to do. You'll feel better after getting rid of it." I hadn't gotten my hands dirty, but I automatically turned to wash them. As I did, Allen's head flopped down to his knees, and he threw up mightily into his underwear, pants, and coveralls.

"Nice shot." I laughed before I could catch myself. The guy was suffering, but I couldn't help being overcome by the comedy of the situation. I righted Allen and said, "Sorry about that," but his head went back down, and he threw up again. *One end or the other*, I thought, washing my hands again. *What a mess.*

There was still an hour left in the shift, enough time to help Allen get cleaned up and out of there. "You wait here, Allen. I'll be back in a minute," I said unnecessarily; Allen wasn't going anywhere. He groaned an answer I didn't understand.

I walked back to the tool room, got some supplies, and returned to the ship, where I cleaned up the magazine compartment. Passing Ollie on the way down, I handed her the timecards. "Give these out at the end of the shift, would you, Ollie? Thanks."

Russell must have filled her in, because Ollie nodded and asked, "He gonna be all right?"

"Yeah, once I get him cleaned up."

Back in the locker room, I found Allen still on the john. He was more alert but tired out. "Sorry, Nolan," was the first thing he said before belching and shaking his head. "I'm feeling better now."

"Let's start by getting your work boots off. Can you undo the laces?" I placed a plastic garbage bag next to him. "Toss your clothes in there, and I'll see if I can find you some new coveralls." Once Allen got his clothes off, I pointed him in the direction of the showers, then went downstairs to grab a fresh pair of white hat Lockheed coveralls from the main yard office.

After hurrying back to the locker room, I set the coveralls on a bench and hollered into the showers, "You get to look like a white hat tonight, Allen." Russell brought up a cup of coffee from the vending machines, and Allen ended the shift basically able to walk on his own, albeit unsteadily. We got him out the gate and into my car, and I dropped him off at his apartment in the Central Area, leaving his laundry at the front door and watching him make his way inside before I headed home.

The crew was back at work the next afternoon, and no one said a word about what happened.

The following week Jacobs shed some light on what lay ahead for us on the *Ray*. "There were some layoffs on day shift."

"Does that mean layoffs on swing too?"

"Well…" He hesitated. "Not today or tomorrow, but somewhere down the line, yeah. Probably next month."

"That's in two weeks. Layoffs or transfers?"

"Could be either. It'll depend on a person's seniority."

"When will we know?"

"We won't know until it happens." He smiled. "That's how Lockheed likes to do things."

"Does this get back to the part about stealing stuff and breaking things on your way out?" I asked with a grin.

"It's just the way they do things," Jacobs said.

It came as no surprise that, two weeks later, I received instructions for a layoff. "Here's a RIF notice." Jacobs handed me a pink slip with the night's work order. "It's for Allen, your guy on work release. Remember, don't give it to him until the end of the shift."

"Right," I said, staring at the paperwork.

"Just hand it to him with his timecard when you wrap up at the end of the night."

"Got it."

I began the shift by meeting the crew on the main deck, collecting timecards and assigning the work for the night. When I got to Allen, I said, "Let's talk," and we stepped away from the gangway. "You can see that the work is winding down on the ship, right, Allen?"

"Is it?" He glanced around.

"Yeah, it is. So we're going to start having some layoffs."

"You mean me? Like, tonight?"

"Yeah." I nodded. "You…tonight. So, look, I'll put you on fire watch. You can take it easy, give yourself time to clean out your locker, then finish out the shift." Allen didn't say anything, just nodded, so I added, "Tomorrow you'll be down at the union hall, and J.J. can send you out on a new job."

"Okay," Allen said, then smiled. "Thanks for telling me now instead of the end of the shift, like they usually do."

"Sure, just keep it between you and me."

He walked to the fantail to get a fire extinguisher, and as he passed me on the way back, he said, "And thanks for the help with that other thing."

"Yeah, well…" I patted him on the back. "Schnapps will do that to you. We'll keep that between you and me, too."

I went to the bow for a smoke. Standing in front of the superstructure and surveying downtown Seattle across Elliott Bay, I thought about where I stood on the seniority list. I had worked my way up for two years and was confident this round of layoffs wouldn't touch me.

Some people thought of the seniority list as being cast in stone, but certain situations would cause it to be fluid. Once in a while someone would quit, but if they continued to pay their union dues, they kept their place on the list. Some guys quit because they got fed up with work, while others left to withdraw retirement pay they had accrued. Still others would go on "voluntary layoff," which—unlike quitting—would allow them to collect unemployment, or "rockin' chair" money, as it was called. All of these situations affected the seniority list and someone's position on it.

Two weeks after Allen left, I received the paperwork to transfer Ollie and Russell to day shift, to new construction on the AS41. They both had years and years of seniority and knew there was no question of being laid off. Their transition was smooth. The week before, though, David was laid off, and his transition was anything but easy.

"You know the work is winding down," I began, as I had with Allen.

"Yeah, I know," David said. "I've been tracking the layoffs on day shift."

"Okay, so you know—"

"I know there are three people on day shift below me on the seniority list," he cut in, his voice rising. "Those guys are supposed to be laid off before me."

"Well," I said, remaining calm, "all I can tell you is the day-shift work order says you're supposed to be riffed tonight."

"No fucking way!" David shouted. He had about four inches and maybe thirty pounds on me, and right then he seemed even bigger. "You can't lay me off out of order, and you know it."

How did this escalate so quickly? "It's not my call, David," I said evenly. "If it's a seniority issue, someone down at the union hall will have to sort it out for you."

"That's fucking bullshit," he yelled and stormed off. I don't know where he went, because we hadn't gotten as far as work assignments for the night.

At lunchtime, I found him smoldering in the locker room and sat down across from him, expecting to talk things out, but he demanded, "Gimme my timecard."

"Okay…" I pulled his card from my pocket, signed it, and handed it to him. "Are you clocking out now?"

"That's for me to decide." He stood, tall and imposing, then turned and stalked away.

Back on board the *Ray*, David was nowhere to be found.

Russell approached me in a passageway. "Nolan, I talked with David. He's mad—real mad." He glanced around to see if anyone could hear us. "He says he's gonna beat the shit outta you."

I straightened my back, and my face tightened as Russell's eyes searched mine.

"Yeah," Russell continued in hushed tones, "when you come out of the gate tonight. He says he'll be waiting for you. He says he's gonna kick your ass."

"Great," I said, trying to regain my composure.

"Look, I'll walk out the gate with you, if you want." He patted me on the shoulder. "I'll walk to your car with you."

I took a deep breath. "No, you don't have to do that. I'll deal with it. Thanks, Russell."

The rest of the shift crawled by, as if the clock refused to move forward. As midnight approached, I gave Russell and Ollie their timecards. David was not on the ship or in the locker room.

Eventually, the whistle blew, and I started out to the gate with a sinking, empty feeling in my stomach I hadn't experienced since I was a kid. My breathing grew heavier; my senses sharpened. My heart pulsed in my chest as if it were trying to beat its way out. Memories of a fist fight back in junior high school came tumbling back to me while the tape in my brain kept replaying, "He's gonna beat the shit outta you."

I began to feel *undiluted fear*. The prospect of getting my face pounded by a man much larger than myself was unnerving, but the idea of that happening while members of my crew stood by and watched was even worse. Fighting a desperate urge to run, my body responded mechanically, with my jaw clenched and my legs robotically moving me toward the gate. I punched my timecard and walked through.

The second I was on the other side, following the last of the swing-shift crowd, my radar confirmed I was no longer safe. The visceral fear centering in my chest pumped through the rest of my body, and my legs and arms tensed. Standing alone, I scanned the cars in the parking lot; most zoomed off into the darkness in less than two minutes. My mouth went dry, and the muscles across my shoulders started to spasm. *This is when it's going to happen. Keep walking.*

I willed myself to move toward my car, my eyes darting around the six or seven remaining vehicles, every shadow becoming the shape of a person. When I reached my car, I automatically held my keys out to unlock the door.

No sound broke the nighttime stillness, the shadows remained shadows, but there was something that didn't measure up. Standing next to my car, I retreated a couple steps and looked at the door lock, but in the half light, I couldn't tell what was wrong. Holding the key at chest level, I approached the car door again, and then I understood. The door seemed a little lower. Taking a step back, I squinted for a moment, then walked around the vehicle. All four tires had been slashed.

CHAPTER 19

"You'll be transferring," Jacobs told me, "but I think it'll be to a different swing-shift assignment." *Perfect.* I'd been expecting the move, but if Lockheed sent me to day shift, I'd have to quit work, with grad school going full bore.

Two nights later, Jacobs asked me to turn in my "L." That wasn't a surprise. As I peeled the sticker off my hard hat, he said with a smile, "At least you get to stay here; you'll be working in the dock office. Actually, you'll be cleaning it."

Fine with me. I went back to being a broom-pushing ship scaler, a crew of one. The job lasted about a month. I cleaned the dock office, the white hat changing room, the bathroom, and any other space that needed cleaning. Sometimes I'd get detailed out to help with a job on the pier or one of the dry docks. The work was low-key, relatively stress-free, and fit in perfectly with my full daytime schedule, now wrapping up my second quarter at school. I even made progress in my love life, having met and started dating a woman who lived in my apartment building. The one thing I missed was my buddy Chris Wells. I hadn't seen him in a while; with our opposite schedules, we rarely crossed paths.

I stayed on swing into the next month, and when I finished early one evening, Jacobs handed me my timecard. "You've got a new assignment coming up next week."

"Am I still on swing shift?" I was fine with being the night custodian and wasn't anxious to make a move.

"Yes," he said firmly. "We've got a Navy vessel, the *Sacramento*, coming into ship repair, and you'll be moved there."

So far, so good.

"And," he continued, "it looks like you'll be getting your 'L' back."

"Really?" My eyebrows arched. I would be happy working for someone else just to stay on swing. I hadn't expected to continue as a leadman.

"Sure. You got my recommendation. You earned it."

"Thanks," I said, shaking his hand.

"You did a good job with your crew on the *Ray*," he said, "like that time you cleaned up after Allen."

That stopped me cold. I looked Jacobs in the eye, and he started to chuckle. I wanted to say, "Now how the hell did you find out about that?" but I kept quiet.

To fill the silence, Jacobs said, "The *Sacramento* is a big mother, a combat support ship that served in Vietnam. It was built over in Bremerton."

"So it's in for..."

"Overhaul and repair, which means it'll be parked here for a while."

"Great."

"Lee Vincent will be the swing-shift supervisor there. Do you know Lee?"

"Sure I do." I had crossed paths with Vincent on other ship repair jobs and knew he was an easygoing type.

"Well, report to him Monday evening, and he'll get you going."

The following Monday, after checking in with Vincent in the makeshift office set up in the *Sacramento*'s wardroom, I eagerly awaited my new crew of six scalers. Clutching the swing-shift work order and a list of the ship scalers on my crew, I scanned through the names and read one that made me smile: Wilfred—a barrel-chested, jovial, slow-moving guy I had worked with as a ship scaler, someone the sandblasters joked about. Dunbar and Eddie told me Wilfred had been a sandblaster but gave it up.

"I was there when it happened," Dunbar said, "swear to god."

"When *what* happened?"

"First"—Dunbar held up a finger—"you gotta understand that Wilfred was not the hardest working sandblaster in the world."

"Okay."

"Sometimes he'd even sneak off and find some place to catch a quick forty winks."

"That's hard to do when you're sandblasting..."

Raising both hands, Eddie added, "Give the man credit for being creative. One time Wilfred was blasting on his own, in some upper-level space, and he decided to tie his hose down and sack out."

"That worked?" I asked.

"*Too* well," Dunbar chuckled.

"He took his hose and tied the motherfucker to a flange on the deck, and kept the trigger down with a wedge," Eddie said.

"How long did he sack out for?"

"*Too* long," Dunbar said, slapping his thigh. "That hose kept blasting away at the deck until it bore a hole clean through."

"No shit?"

"Worst part was that Wilfred was blasting above the wardroom the white hats had converted into an office." Now Dunbar was laughing. "All them white hats got themselves a good shower of sand. Cleared out the wardroom in a hurry. And that was the end of Wilfred's sandblasting career."

"They didn't fire him?" I asked.

"No," Eddie said, "that motherfucker has a long tongue."

"It's not what you know," Dunbar said. "It's who you blow."

Later on, I asked Espy if the story was true.

"Oh, hell no," Espy said, shaking his head. "That son of a bitch gave up sandblasting because he was lazy, that's all."

"Hmmm…I thought it sounded too good to be true."

Espy looked off in the distance and arched his brows. "Makes a hell of a story, though."

I smiled, thinking back to a conversation I did have with him about my experiences trying to get signed up at the ship scaler's union hall. I told Wilfred about how I was desperate enough to sleep out on the sidewalk in front of the hall, in the middle of the night, so I'd be first in line for the early morning job call from J.J.

"Oh hell, Nolan," he told me, "don't you know nothin'?" Wilfred had a high-pitched, squeaky voice, and I could tell he enjoyed setting the White boy straight.

"All you gotta do, Nolan, is go 'round back the union hall, knock on the door, and hand J.J. a fifth." He threw his head back laughing, as his round belly shook. "That old son of a bitch drinks like a fish. Didn't you know that?"

It would be fun having Wilfred on the crew, for comic relief if nothing else. I never did ask him about the sandblasting incident.

The whistle blew, and a couple minutes later some ship scalers approached the *Sacramento*. The first two up the gangway were Mexican-American brothers, George and Steve Rodriguez, whom I had worked with once before in ship repair. Next came Wilfred, who laughed and shook my hand; then two White women, Gina and Lilly; followed by a tall, long-haired White guy named O'Connor.

"Okay, let's get to work," I said, reminding myself of the rules of management I had learned: treat people with dignity, the same way I want to be treated; give them the work; and get out of the way.

I spent the next two hours checking up on each job site and exploring the rest of the ship in between. At one point I ran into Vincent. "Jacobs tells me good things about you," he said.

"Come on, Lee, you already knew that." We both laughed.

"Yeah," he said, "just get through the work order every night, and you'll keep the people on day shift happy." *And keep Lee Vincent happy too*, I thought to myself.

My crew represented a real cross-section of the working population in the shipyard. White males still dominated the other crafts, but African Americans made up the majority of the ship scalers. There were Asians too, mostly Vietnamese, in both the Ship Scalers and the Painters Union, as well as a handful of Hispanics.

The more I got to know George and Steve Rodriguez, the more I concluded that these two were the hardest working men I'd ever met. From what I could tell, that aspect of shipbuilding culture seemed colorblind: if a person worked hard and got the job done, nothing else mattered. Race took a back seat to a person's work ethic. Looking back now, I'm sure I saw the world through rose-colored glasses. Racism in the early 1980s was alive and well, even if—as a White guy—I didn't look closely enough to pick up on the outward signs of it.

In what seemed like a reversal of discrimination, I remember Davis telling me about a crew he had organized once on day shift. "Yeah, I put me together a crew once that was all *Vietnam-ease.* Damn hard workers," Davis said fondly, shaking his head. "Good crew. Got a hell of a lot done." Then he shrugged. "Didn't last, though."

"What happened?" I asked.

"Oh, you know…same old shit. Some damn fool white hat found out about it and busted the crew up." Davis rolled his eyes. "Racial thing, I guess. Too bad."

The only racial divisions I was aware of were the ones we made for ourselves. Everyone—Black, White, Asian, Hispanic—worked together and interacted on the job, but during lunch most people sorted themselves out. Black guys hung out with other Black guys, Whites with Whites, and there was always a table of men speaking Vietnamese at lunch. Exceptions existed, of course, but usually people identified with a group.

I did my best to connect with people and try to understand where they were coming from, but even though I was the guy with a college degree, I still had a long way to travel in terms of appreciating other people's culture and background. One night on the *Sacramento*, I recall asking Steve Rodriguez, "If you and your brother are from Mexico, how come you've got names like George and Steve?"

Steve stopped what he was doing and looked directly at me. "Our names are Jorge and Esteban," he said evenly, without a trace of malice. Then he added, "We use George and Steve to make it easier for people like you."

"Oh...okay," I acknowledged.

That moment stayed with me, enough so that I started to appreciate how important it was for me to try a little harder, to go beyond myself to try to appreciate where other people are coming from. I needed to extend myself.

I look back today and know that what I learned in the shipyard—what essentially became my second education—didn't only affect how I saw myself; it changed how I saw the people around me. What did the Rodriguez brothers go through to get here? What about men like Eddie or Espy or Dunbar—guys who were hardworking and bright and dedicated to their craft? What did they have to go through just to get this far? And how might their lives have been different if they had started off with some of the advantages I began with as a kid?

Growing up during the Civil Rights movement of the 1960s, I thought of myself as someone who appreciated cultural and racial differences. I loved soul music and followed artists like James Brown, Aretha Franklin, and the Temptations. I read *To Kill a Mockingbird* and *The Autobiography of Malcolm X*. For myself, and maybe for many White males, it was easy to conflate an appreciation of Black music and culture with an understanding of what it's like to be Black and to be subjected to racism all your life. Looking back, I see how far off the mark I was. I never really thought about the Black experience in America on a personal level, or about systemic racism. Even though I was the only White blaster on the sandblasting crew, I never intentionally tried to feel a Black individual's experience of what it must be like interacting with a large group of White people every single day at work.

George and Steve were magnanimous men who, at least on the outside, accepted my sheltered background and lack of cultural understanding. They always kept things low-key, and when we interacted, I felt invited into their circle. Once, in the locker room, George was changing at the end of the shift. The guy was built like a bull, and when his shirt came off, he had the cut look of a serious weight lifter. He was also heavily tattooed. A royal flush poker hand decorated one shoulder, and a weeping Madonna was on his chest. When George caught me staring, he turned his other shoulder, and I was looking down the barrel of a .45. He flexed, which stretched the gun a little, then flashed a grin. "Don't worry, it's not loaded."

Regarding racism and discrimination, all I honestly know is how I was treated. When I was the minority on the sandblasting crew, I never felt marginalized or humiliated or made fun of. Throughout my five years in the shipyard, Black ship scalers helped the White guy, Mike Nolan—Brother Nols—every step of the way. They didn't need to, but they did. Lamar befriended me and made it easy for me to fit in on Carol's crew. Richards took me under his wing when I lied about being a sandblaster. He kept me from getting fired and took the time to mentor me. L. T. McQuay guided me with his affable, upbeat manner. And Eddie helped me learn the sandblasting trade, even though it meant taking on extra work until I could figure out what the hell I was doing.

I'll never know the discrimination those men faced in their lives—I never thought to ask—but I know how they treated me. Taking my personal experience in the shipyard in the late 1970s and applying it to American culture today, I can say this: If Whites in America treated Blacks the way Black people treated me in the shipyard, America would be a different place. America would be a better place. We could make society, our country, a more noble place.

CHAPTER 20

Fifty-two Americans were being held hostage in Iran, and there was a sense of anger and anxiety across the country, but Lee Vincent managed to keep things light and breezy at work. He possessed a naturally laid-back style that centered everyone on the lower end of the stress scale. "Oh, it'll all get done," was something he'd say when we hadn't gotten everything done. "Don't worry, we'll still get to heaven," was another favorite saying, usually following some sort of royal fuckup. By nature, I was more anxious than Lee, so being around him was a good influence, showing me how to keep everything in perspective.

Outside of work, I wrapped up my first year of grad school and was ready to enjoy a break from classes during summer quarter. I'd been dating a woman from my apartment complex, and we had settled into an ongoing relationship. Finally, I wasn't desperately trying to figure out plans every weekend; I had someone to be with on a regular basis, someone whose company I enjoyed.

In the meantime, my friend Chris had received some crushing news. The Carter administration decided that the United States would boycott the Summer Olympic Games, in protest of Russia's invasion of Afghanistan. I expected Chris to be devastated, but he showed his mettle. "When you get knocked down," Chris said, "you pick yourself back up, brush yourself off, and keep going. I'll train for the 1984 Olympics." That was Chris. He never said another word about it; Chris just kept on training.

Beyond having someone to date, and connecting with Chris from time to time, my social life consisted mostly of seeing either graduate students at UW or former college friends who were hot on the trail of their Corporate America careers. I envied these up-and-coming professionals, and our encounters only highlighted my feeling of living a double life, socializing in the white-collar world of young urban professionals—"yuppies," as they were beginning to be called—and the blue-collar world of heavy construction, where I lived eight hours every day. The individuals who populated these two worlds didn't overlap, but I found myself blending characteristics of both environments to make up who I was—although *blend* probably wasn't the right word, since the two worlds were so different from each other.

As a college graduate, my backstory was very similar to that of the young professionals, but the connection didn't go any deeper than that. The bond felt superficial, because I was still unsure of my career trajectory. There were plans and hopes and aspirations, but that was all I had. Nothing tangible.

The blue-collar world filled in the gaps. Being a sandblaster in the shipyard provided a clear identity, projecting an image of strength and confidence and just a little bit of swagger. The beautiful thing was, I could feel the power of all these qualities while hanging out with my college buddies, dressed in ordinary street clothes, looking like everybody else. The two worlds made up competing parts of my personality. There was a little tension there, but I was becoming more and more adept at tapping into one or the other, depending on what circumstances called for at the moment.

Occasionally I hung out with the guys from work after the eight-hour shift. One afternoon I got together with Dunbar and Eddie at the Blew Eagle Tavern, conveniently situated just off the West Seattle Bridge. Dark and smoky, lit by beer signs, the place was always animated and loud, crowded with guys ready for a drink or two at the end of their work day. Broken glass on the floor crunched under our work boots as we made our way to the bar to order a drink, walking around some guy who'd actually ridden his chopper up the tavern steps and into the bar. Yes, there are two different worlds that I live in.

Over a few beers, the conversation with Eddie and Dunbar turned to business at Lockheed. "Three Navy contracts for three sub tenders is in the bag. There's talk about a fourth," Eddie said, "but that'd be the end of it."

"I heard there might be a new class of ferries built," Dunbar said.

"No," Eddie countered. "I mean, yeah, there's supposed to be a new ferry contract out there somewhere, but I heard it was goin' to Todd."

"Why do we only build Navy ships and ferry boats?" I asked. "What about cargo ships or oil tankers or cruise liners?" My question stopped the conversation, and the attention turned to me. "I mean, there's a market for that, right?"

"It's *all* about the market," Eddie answered. "We can compete with other shipyards along the West Coast, and even with the big shipyards back East. But along the gulf—Florida, Alabama, Louisiana,

Texas—the wages are lower. Makes it way harder for us to compete."

"They underbid us," Dunbar added, "but even *they* get underbid by shipyards in other countries."

"That's right," Eddie said. "Them other ships you mentioned, oil tankers and cargo ships, they all get built overseas these days. That's where the wages are the lowest—Japan, you know, South Korea, places like that."

"Hell…they underbid American shipyards every time," Dunbar added.

"I guess if I was the one paying for it," I said, "I'd look for the shipyard that could build the cheapest." Again, the conversation stopped, and I looked around the table, wondering if I'd said the wrong thing. "I mean… that makes sense, right?"

"Time was," Dunbar continued, picking up the thread, "we had the edge in shipbuilding." He shrugged. "Not anymore."

"Japan caught up with us," Eddie said. "You'd buy a watch or maybe a camera from Japan, wouldn't you?"

"They say those Japanese are damn hard workers." Dunbar sipped his beer. "Cheap too, which means we don't get no more private contracts, only government contracts."

"You know…the last private contract we had was eight years ago, the sugar ship," Eddie said.

"The what?"

"It was called the *Sugar Islander*," Dunbar said, "a big bulk freighter we built for the C&H Sugar Company."

"We built a couple icebreakers for the Coast Guard," Eddie added, "but Lockheed hasn't built nothing commercial since the sugar ship."

"So that leaves us with Navy contracts?"

"Navy, Coast Guard, and Washington State," Dunbar answered.

"Washington State ferries won't be built nowhere 'cept Washington State," Eddie added.

"So that means our competition is just Todd," Dunbar said, "at least for them state ferries. Navy and Coast Guard means we're competing all along the coast, East Coast too, and 'specially on the Gulf Coast. All them shipyards…"

"So, as long as we're making a better wage than those guys, there's a pretty good chance we're not going to get contracts, right?" I said.

Again, no one responded. Somehow, I managed to stop the conversation every time I opened my mouth, and it occurred to me that maybe this would be a good time to keep my mouth closed. I probably wouldn't work in the shipyard forever—this was an in-between place for me—but these guys were here to stay. That realization caused a subtle sense of distance between me and Eddie and Dunbar, and made me feel guilty. This was their livelihood, their future. I'd put in my time and worked hard to be part of the crew, to become "one of the guys" and earn their acceptance as a fellow sandblaster, but the self-confidence that resulted from that acceptance only pushed me in a different direction. Ironically, the more I established myself in the blue-collar world of shipbuilding, the less it felt like a home for me.

As Eddie and Dunbar sipped their beer, I considered the bigger picture. My thoughts turned to the Joint Metal Trades contract, and I wondered when it would be up for negotiation. We had good-paying jobs...the American Dream was accessible right here at Lockheed Shipyard, through the Ship Scalers Union. Anyone could walk into the union hall—no connections, no strings being pulled, no money changing hands under the table—and latch on to a high-wage union job, with benefits. Anyone could sign on as a laborer, unskilled and untrained, and pursue the dream.

I thought about the old-timers in the shipyard; most of them probably *were* living the American Dream. They showed up every day, worked hard, and now owned homes in West Seattle or the Central Area. These were men who never missed a day of work, and they weren't asking for a lot, either: a decent wage, health benefits, enough money to pay the mortgage—maybe the opportunity to send their kid to college, and then after working forty years, to retire.

For the next generation coming up behind me, would the American Dream stick around? Would someone find it here at Lockheed Shipyard? Based on this conversation, it didn't look too promising. If shipping lines and cruise companies were taking their construction dollars overseas, it seemed doubtful that the current level of American shipbuilding could maintain its viability—certainly not on the world stage.

In a few years, things *would* change. I left the shipyard in the spring of 1984, two years before the struggle over a new contract began. In 1986, the union and the shipyard were miles apart in negotiations, disagreeing not only on wages but also on changes the company wanted to make regarding seniority and benefits. Following fruitless discussions, the shipyard locked out the workers. The Ship Scalers Union folded later that year, and Lockheed Shipyard closed for good in 1988. Todd Shipyard filed for bankruptcy in 1987, then stabilized itself and was sold to Vigor Shipbuilding in 2010.

Today there aren't as many blue-collar opportunities to walk into the way I did, although there are still laborers involved in shipbuilding. The laborers union I belonged to is now based in Tacoma, where they provide training and an apprenticeship program, and the pay starts at $22.36 an hour. But to sign on, you need a written referral, and there are fewer jobs because there are fewer shipyards. The path to the American Dream is not as wide or as easy to enter as it once was.

At the Blew Eagle Tavern, the conversation with Eddie and Dunbar confirmed my realization that shipbuilding was probably not a viable long-term job option, at least not for me, even if I had *wanted* to stay.

Working aboard the *Sacramento*, I appreciated what I had. Being swing-shift leadman was a breeze, and the job would last for months while the ship was being overhauled. And my crew was solid: a group of contrasting personalities who all happened to get along. During my months on the *Sacramento*, no one on my crew ever ended up in any of those "auto-matic termin-nation" situations, but Wilfred did inform me about one that happened to someone else on day shift.

"You remember Sal, back on the AS39?" he asked me.

"Surc I do. Everyone knows Sal."

"They had him fire watchin' somewhere on the ship. I'm not sure where, maybe down in the boiler room. Anyway, Sal had himself parked on a five-gallon bucket, sitting next to his fire extinguisher, dark glasses on and dead to the world."

"Sal's favorite job," I observed. "Was he drunk or asleep?"

"He was sober," Wilfred answered, "but the leadman walks by, and Sal never moves."

"Sal wouldn't move with the ship burning down," I said.

"The leadman walks by again, then waves a glove in front of Sal's face. He knows ol' Sal is fast asleep, so he goes and gets a white hat as a witness."

"Did Sal wake up in time?"

"Nope. The white hat does the same thing, waving his arms in front of Sal's face. When he don't move, the white hat figures they got him, *with witnesses*, sleeping on the job." Wilfred started laughing. "So with Sal sitting there, not moving, the white hat shakes him by the shoulder and tells him he's fired for sleeping on the job."

"Something tells me Sal wiggled out of it..."

"Well, ol' Sal is smarter than most people give him credit for."

"Okay," I admitted, "lazy but smart. What happened?"

"Sal stands up in front of that white hat," Wilfred said, now standing, "an' he crosses himself." With a wide grin on his face, Wilfred reached up and touched his forehead, his chest, and both shoulders. "You know, like they do in church."

"I don't believe it," I said, laughing.

"Swear to god, and then Sal says, 'Amen,' and tells the white hat that he was prayin'."

"What happened next?"

"Turns out they can't fire you for prayin'," Wilfred said. "Sal was gone a couple days while the union met with Lockheed and sorted it all out. Then he was back at work."

"Good ol' Sal." I shook my head. "They'll never get rid of him."

"The union got him reinstated," Wilfred explained, "plus back pay for the two days he was out."

"I'm sure Sal's a very religious guy."

"It got me prayin'," Wilfred answered.

On the opposite end of the work scale were the hard-charging Rodriguez brothers. A white hat must have noticed their work ethic, because they were transferred from my crew to another vessel in ship repair, and Steve was made a leadman on day shift. Even so, the brothers' story took an unexpected turn a couple months later. One night, George was working on the dry dock in ship repair when four men showed up wearing suits. Lee Vincent filled me in on what happened.

"You know we don't see suits around here," Lee said, "so when these four guys appeared, we figured something was going down."

"Did you know the guys?" I asked.

"At first I thought they were Lockheed management, you know, higher ups," Lee said, "but none of them looked familiar."

"So who were they?"

"I figured it out when they flashed their badges."

"Oh."

"Yeah. I was standing on the pier with four FBI agents, and they were looking for George Rodriguez."

"What happened?"

"I told them George was working under the barge, down on the dry dock." Lee pointed over his shoulder. "Those guys looked at the dry dock floating in the water and said, 'That'll make it easier.' What they meant was, there's no place for George to go, unless he's a damn good swimmer."

"Did they take him away?"

Lee nodded. "In handcuffs. Turns out George escaped from a prison a few years ago somewhere in the Southwest, and the FBI had been looking for him ever since. George was cuffed and escorted out the gate."

I never saw George again, but his brother Steve kept working on day shift as a leadman. On my crew, the Rodriguez brothers had been replaced by Jerry, a White guy about the same age as me, and Marcus, a Black guy with a Jamaican accent. They weren't the Rodriguez brothers, but they were still good workers and fit in well with Gina, Lilly, O'Connor, and Wilfred—who I almost killed one night.

I had gone through the swing-shift work order and assigned Wilfred the job of cleaning an elevator shaft. "It's a service elevator, running from the main deck to the third deck. Come on, Wilfred, let's go take a look at it."

Wilfred followed me down three decks to look for the elevator. The *Sacramento* had gigantic cargo elevators, large enough to drive a truck into, but also several smaller service elevators, more like dumbwaiters, used to move tools or parts.

"Here we go." The bottom of the elevator shaft was about three feet by four feet square. "Check out that grease." I pointed around the elevator cables running along the inside of the shaft.

"That's what I'll start on," Wilfred said.

"Right. Why don't you go to the tool room and get some degreaser, and I'll go aloft and check out the upper part of the shaft."

I went back to the main deck and found the elevator carriage, which also needed cleaning, then went down one deck and looked at the walls of the shaft. At the level of each deck was a four-inch sill that would need to be wiped down too, and someone had propped a 2-by-3-foot, half-inch-thick steel plate on it that would need to be moved. With one foot on the deck and the other braced on a side of the sill, I leaned into the open shaft for the steel plate. Wilfred was working at the bottom of the shaft floor, busy with a spray gun and degreaser.

Stretching my arm, I could just get my hands on the plate's upper edges. Slowly, I tilted the plate up and off the sill. I don't know why I thought I could hold a piece of steel that size without getting underneath it—it weighed well over a hundred pounds. The moment I lifted the plate off the sill—*swoosh!*—it slipped right through my gloved hands, straight down the shaft.

"*WILFRED*," I screamed as the plate sliced through the air like a guillotine blade. It smashed into the bottom of the shaft with a metallic crash that echoed through the ship. Wide-eyed and breathing uncontrollably, I searched below. *I killed Wilfred.*

That's when Wilfred slowly poked his head back into the shaft. "It's okay, Nolan," he hollered. "I saw you movin' that steel plate…"

It was a long cigarette break out on the bow before my hands quit shaking and my heart rate slowed down. Stories about accidents and injuries cropped up from time to time, but they felt detached, as if they happened somewhere else. I remember hearing about two Vietnamese painters killed on the job. They had just finished spraying a compartment and decided to have a cigarette break, but they lit up too close to the space and ignited the paint fumes. A fireball enveloped them, and they both died later that night in an emergency room.

Well, they should have known better than to light up so close to the fumes, I thought. I always came up with an explanation or excuse after the fact. But shipyard injuries and deaths happened without the benefit of 20-20 hindsight. I came *that close* to killing Wilfred. It was always an ordinary situation: someone doing their job and something unexpectedly going wrong, out of the blue. I heard one welder say fatalistically, "That's part of working in heavy construction. Any place like this will always have injuries." He shrugged his shoulders. "There are more fatalities workin' construction than in any other line of work."

I knew it, but I tried not to dwell on it. I told myself to be careful, hoping that would be enough. Obviously, it wasn't. Wilfred could have died in that elevator shaft.

A month later, in June, I was asleep in my apartment when the phone rang, between 1:00 and 2:00 in the morning. A little groggy, I made my way from my bedroom to the living room, then picked up the phone and cleared my throat. "Hello?"

"Is this Mike Nolan?"

I blinked and coughed. "Yes."

"Chris Wells is dead."

CHAPTER 21

hat?”

“Chris Wells is dead.” It was O’Connor, a scaler from my crew.

“No, he’s not.”

“Chris Wells is dead,” O’Connor repeated. He knew Chris and I were good friends. “He died at work today.”

“Are you sure?” This was unbelievable. “That can’t be right.”

“Yes, I’m sure. I heard about it at the end of the shift today.”

“Are you certain it was Wells who died?” O’Connor *must* have it wrong. I refused to believe it was Chris.

The conversation went back and forth, but eventually we stopped talking and hung up. I sat there in my apartment, repeating what O’Connor told me, trying to make sense of it. I laid back in bed, but couldn’t fall asleep. On top of the covers, eyes wide open in the dark, I forced myself to close my eyes and try to sleep. All I could picture was Chris. Uncomprehending but wide awake, I got up and made myself some coffee, then waited for the sun to rise.

That afternoon, Lee Vincent explained what had happened. “He was working on the AS40, in the cab of the kingpin crane. Wells was cleaning the floor.”

I remember working around that thirty-ton crane and could picture the cab. Chris would have needed to crouch down under the control panel to do the cleaning; he must have felt confined in that tight space.

“I think he was working around the foot pedals, cleaning with Nacolene, and was overcome by fumes.”

“What do you mean ‘overcome’?”

“There was air to breathe in the cab,” Lee explained, “but the fumes from Nacolene are heavier than air, so as he worked the fumes eventually settled into the lower part of the cab and displaced the oxygen.” He shook his head. “Since Nacolene is odorless, Wells wouldn’t have noticed he was breathing the fumes. He was asphyxiated.”

"Where the hell was Thompson, the safety guy?"

"Good question," Lee said, frowning.

That was all I could listen to. I took the work order from Vincent and went out to the main deck to wait for the shift to begin.

As my crew gathered around me, I was numb, trying to keep the image of Chris dying out of my mind. Going through the tasks on the work order made me picture every possible way someone could get killed, every single way something could go wrong. Someone on my crew could be working, just like Chris, and suddenly there would be an accident they'd never see coming. *I* would never see it coming.

"Okay…job assignments for tonight." My back straightened as I tried to push the images out of my mind. "Gina, Lilly, and Wilfred, I need you three to muck out bilges in the engine room." The three of them groaned, but I didn't care.

After I'd given out the rest of the jobs, everyone headed off to work. I spent the first part of the shift trying to stay busy with checking up on the crew, but when I went to the fantail for a cigarette, my mind was still fixed on Chris in that kingpin crane.

Normally, for a job involving Nacolene, one or two ventilation lines would have been run into that cab. Why hadn't that happened? I imagined the heavy Nacolene fumes settling to the bottom of the cab as Chris worked away to clean the grease, never noticing what was happening. The colorless fumes would have put their deadly fingers around Chris's face, covering his mouth and nose. He would have felt a little tired or sluggish, or even slightly lightheaded, then he would have fallen asleep. A gentle, drowsy slumber, leading Chris to a painless death.

Squeezing the fantail railing, I rocked forward and back, then wiped my cheeks with the back of my hand. I lit another cigarette. My heart ached for my friend, and I was angry. Angry at his leadman, who should have checked on him; angry at the ventilation guy for not setting up the job right; and angry at Chris for dying, crazy as that sounds. The magnitude of his life ending pushed down on me. We were both young guys, hustling to make things work out while keeping an eye optimistically on the future, and Chris was a lot closer to making his future dreams come true than I was. He was on a path, Chris was going somewhere, and he had accomplished so much. "Nothing is guaranteed," I said, shaking my head, "and it doesn't matter who you are or how hard you try."

Grieving Chris's death left me empty, the sadness draining my energy. The mental image of Chris lying dead in that crane was the opposite of how I thought of Chris: optimistic, outgoing, a guy filled with promise and overflowing possibilities. Chris kept all that energy in with a barely suppressed grin, telegraphing his confidence to anyone around him. Life was supposed to be an adventure, and if it wasn't, Chris would do his best to turn it into one. The Chris I wanted to remember kept going in and out of my mind, changing places with the image of the dead Chris.

What would he want me to do at this point? Chris would tell me to put my chin up and shake it off. I could hear his voice: "Let's get going, Nolan. Get your ass in gear!" That's what Chris would say. I silently nodded, at the same time thinking, *I gotta get out of here.* Sticking around here and assuming I wouldn't get injured or killed was not an option anymore.

Over the next two or three weeks, people asked me about Chris, talked about the funeral, and speculated about possible legal action the union might take against the shipyard. A month after his death, however, the work routine went back to normal, and after that people mentioned Chris less and less. But a day rarely went by that I didn't think about him, and the image of Chris's body lying in the bottom of that crane cab kept pointing me to the exit.

CHAPTER 22

That fall marked the beginning of my second year in graduate school. I continued as a swing-shift leadman on the *Sacramento*, occasionally sneaking a book in my coveralls to surreptitiously study. Between school and work, I was constantly on the run, sometimes showing up to class in dirty coveralls, usually exhausted. But when winter quarter started, I had a class every Wednesday morning in which there was no possibility of falling asleep.

The class was small, as upper-level grad classes often are, with six or eight people. The course began with the professor introducing herself, reviewing the class syllabus, then inviting everyone to take turns saying where they did their undergraduate work and mentioning something about themselves. The first person to take the podium was Ann, an attractive, brown-eyed girl from Minnesota. As she spoke, I sensed a connection with her, especially when Ann mentioned she had attended Gonzaga; even though it was a small campus, we had never crossed paths there. After teaching a few years, Ann had enrolled in graduate school and, like me, was finishing up her master's.

I was the last to speak. Standing behind the podium, I mentioned being a native Washingtonian, working in West Seattle, and doing my undergraduate work at Gonzaga. For that last part, I waited a beat and made eye contact with the girl from Minnesota. Other people must have been thinking about us, too, because, unbeknownst to me, one of Ann's girlfriends passed her a note: *You have a lot in common with this boy. Go for it!*

After class ended, I caught up with Ann in the hallway and tried hard to play it cool. "So, you attended Gonzaga?"

"Yes, that's where I got my teaching certificate."

"Well," I said, "we'll have to get together sometime and talk about GU over coffee."

"Sure…I'd like that."

I was attracted to her right away, but months of searching for romance had taught me that the harder I aimed for a target, the more likely I was to miss it. I finally understood that relationships need to happen on their own. So when I met Ann, we started off as friends.

I was still dating the woman who lived in my apartment complex. She was beautiful, vivacious, and stylish, but we had been together for a while now, and I knew we were never going to progress beyond dinner and staying over for the night. It was a nice relationship with a wonderful person, but it wasn't *the* relationship. As much as I enjoyed her company, I never saw the two of us as anything more than that.

In January 1982, the UW football team was heading to Pasadena to face Iowa in the Rose Bowl. As a student, I could get tickets, so I convinced my dad that we should fly to California on New Year's and go to the game. My girlfriend from the apartment complex was busy, so I asked my friend from Minnesota if she would drive us to the airport. The three of us talked the whole way.

When my dad and I settled into our flight, he told me, "That girl who drove us—Ann—is terrific. You should get to know her." Although I was involved with someone else, something told me he was right. I got together with Ann for coffee, then we met for lunch, and after that we went out to dinner.

During the next few weeks the other relationship melted away, as I saw less of my girlfriend and more of Ann. It was easy, because Ann was so much fun to be around. A long-distance runner, Ann was an active, outdoorsy person, and I got caught up in her activities. She was a member of the Mountaineers, loved hiking and backpacking, and canoed competitively as part of the Seattle Canoe Club. I took up running with Ann, and we started canoeing and hiking together. By the end of winter quarter, we were spending all our free time together.

Meanwhile, work aboard the *Sacramento* was sailing along. No emergencies. I didn't fall out of the crow's nest or have to clean up anyone's drunken vomit. No one slashed my tires. The bullshit was kept to a minimum, and I was able to balance a hectic schedule.

I came to work early one afternoon and crossed paths with Lamar in the locker room. "Yo, Brother Nols. You still goin' to school?" he asked. "You learning to read and write?"

"You could say that," I said, smiling. "I'm still in school, and I'm busting my ass doing it, but I'm getting there. I'll graduate this spring."

"Then what?"

"Then I leave Lockheed and find a job somewhere as a school counselor."

"Right on," Lamar said. "You gonna get a *real* job, know what I mean?" He waved his hand through the air. "Get the hell out of this place." Lamar brought his hand down, slapping mine. "Brother Nols, school counselor!"

I grinned.

"A job where you can be *clean*," Lamar continued, "and for sure you won't miss this bullshit."

"This bullshit got me this far," I admitted, shrugging good-naturedly. "I needed to go through it to get to the other side."

Lamar nodded. "And you came out smelling like a rose."

"We'll see what happens with a new job. I'll try not to stink it up." Then I smiled. "Remember Carol's crew? When I arrived there, I was lost. I didn't know where I was going or what I was doing. You helped me out. I've gotten to the point where I know what I'm doing. I know how to relax. If someone asks where I'm heading, I say, 'I'll tell you when I get there.' That's good enough."

Lamar patted me on the back. "And that's all you *need* to tell them. Hell, Nolan, you figured out how to be a sandblaster and not kill yourself doing it." We both laughed, thinking back to me dangling from the mast of the *Roark*. "I knew you got what it takes ever since I seen you 'yeah, yeah, yeah' old Carol. You'll do fine whatever job you get."

Now I slapped Lamar's hand. "Thanks for helping me get through it all."

"Glad to."

I paused for a second, then said, "You did more than that..." We stood there, looking at each other, communicating without saying a thing. Then I shook his hand and Lamar nodded, turned, and left. I made my way down to the *Sacramento*.

Lamar's words, especially "you got what it takes," stuck with me. I knew most ship scalers would probably prefer doing something different, especially the scalers who were not sandblasters. Who wants to be a laborer all their lives? But the thought of *"being clean and avoiding the bullshit"* didn't tell the whole story. Not mine, anyway. Though my line of work was dirty and dangerous—and got anonymously lumped together with a hundred other construction jobs the general public knew nothing about—I wasn't about to dismiss this place. I owed the shipyard a debt of gratitude. It had gotten me this far, as I told Lamar, and wherever my next job took me, I'd retain the dignity and self-confidence I'd acquired here. I wasn't about to let go of that. I needed it in order to be who I was.

My mind returned to Carol Garcia's crew, to Lamar and Esther befriending me and helping me fit in, to Bob and Vinny and—yes—the "yeah, yeah, yeah" treatment I gave Carol. I'd come a long way since then. When I arrived in Seattle, I was a "lost lammy," frantically searching for work and searching for myself. My reinvention from a nerdy science major to a blue-collar heavy construction worker happened out of desperation, but it forced me to grow. Becoming a sandblaster built me up; the work empowered me to project assurance, confidence, and strength. My "second education" involved much more than learning a craft; this journey had given me an identity.

My dad once said, "It's not what you do; it's who you are." Now I understood what he meant. Maybe that was what had made Chris Wells such a special person. Even before he made the Olympic Team, before he became the "zesty waiter," Chris had had that spark, that enthusiasm and confidence that made me believe he could take on anything in life and conquer it.

I wished Chris could have seen me wrap up at the University of Washington. Though my bachelor's degree hadn't helped me land a job initially, that piece of paper had opened the door to graduate school. I would finish my program with a "job ready" master's degree, leave the shipyard, then reinvent myself all over again as a guidance counselor. This time it was a conscious decision, not a choice made out of desperation. I was in charge. I wanted it, and my shipyard re-creation had given me the willpower to make it happen. Meeting the crew by the gangway, I handed out jobs to everyone. Judging by the kind of work we were doing that night, the *Sacramento*'s overhaul was coming to an end. I mentioned this to Vincent when I returned to the ship's office.

"Yeah," he said, "the *Sacramento* is scheduled to be back in service by the end of next month."

"Then what?"

"Well, there's talk of a frigate coming in for maintenance and repairs, but so far it's just talk."

"What's the alternative?"

Vincent paused and smiled. "I know you want to stay on swing shift, Nolan." He shrugged his shoulders. "There's always the LSD."

He wasn't talking about psychedelic drugs. LSD stood for "landing ship dock," a large Naval vessel that had a "well dock" in the stern of the ship from which amphibious vehicles could be launched. Lockheed Shipbuilding came out ahead in the bidding wars and was awarded the LSD contract just as the third sub tender was being delivered to the Navy. The company had already begun construction on the USS *Whidbey Island*, the first of three LSD vessels.

"Right now they're assembling LSD modules in Yard One and there isn't much of a night shift, but there's room to grow." Vincent patted me on the shoulder. "You're still in school during the day, huh?"

"Yeah, winter quarter. Then one more after that." I wanted to stay on swing shift until the end of spring.

A month later, the *Sacramento* was turned over to the Navy, and most of my crew was sent to day shift. It was a surprise, and a relief, to find I was kept on swing shift as leadman, working out of the ship repair dock office.

Vessels continued to come and go through ship repair, and different scalers were assigned to my crew, depending on the work that needed to be done. Sometimes the ships were in dry dock; other times we made repairs pier-side. My crew would last a few days, a week, or maybe even two weeks, depending on the repairs. There were some familiar faces, but for jobs that only lasted a day or two, I always had new scalers: people trying to get their foot in the door and earn their seniority, just like me when I started out.

Vessels in dry dock sometimes required sandblasting, and then my crew would be my old sandblasting buddies—a fun but humbling experience for me, being in charge of the old pros. I'd hand the work order to Espy or Eddie and say, "You guys know what to do...just let me know if you need anything."

One night I had a ship scaler assigned to me who was more than just a familiar face. We had a tanker in dry dock, and my work order involved a crew of six. As usual, I met people at the start of the shift down on the pier, by the ship's gangway.

"Hello, Nolan" came the gruff voice as he handed me his timecard. It was the Warden, but he didn't have the "F" on his hard hat.

"What are you doing here?" I asked.

"Working for you, I guess."

The rest of the crew lined up next to Hildebrand, and I collected timecards and got the other five scalers started. Once they were out of the way, I had a smoke and spoke with the Warden.

"So, how did you end up here?" I asked.

"Oh, you know, just part of the ups and downs of shipbuilding." That was Hildebrand: matter of fact and to the point. I sensed he didn't like being here, but the Warden would be the last person to whine about it. "The third sub tender was delivered to the Navy in July," he went on, "and I was the last ship scaler to leave the ship."

"No more foreman?"

"You know how it works... people are transferred or get laid off as construction winds down, and you don't need a chief after you get rid of all the Indians." He shrugged. "That's just part of shipbuilding."

"So what do they have you doing now?"

"I'm on a skeleton crew over in new construction, mostly doing yard maintenance. We don't have anything going on tonight, so they sent me here. Once the *Whidbey Island* makes it over from Yard One, we'll get busy again, and I'll probably get my 'F' back."

I felt this encounter brought me full circle in the shipyard, with the Warden working for *me*. I let my cigarette fall and crushed it out. "Well, I'm sure you'll get your "F" back. You're a good foreman. Hell, they *have* to give it back—you're 'The Warden.'"

Hildebrand laughed. I gave him a fire-watch job and went to the bow of the tanker for another smoke. With winter quarter winding down, Ann was now the main focus of my life. We had spent enough time together for me to realize that we were on the same wavelength regarding marriage, work-life balance, wanting to raise a family, and where we wanted to live. Ann was a kindred spirit and she also brought a sense of adventure to our relationship.

Ann maintained an apartment on Queen Anne Hill but was spending less and less time there, moving into my apartment in stages. One day she left a toothbrush in my bathroom. The next week she brought her makeup case. The following week I cleared out half the drawers in the bedroom for her clothes.

No family members knew Ann and I were living together. Both of us came from traditional middle-class Catholic families, so we told our parents we "were involved with someone" and left it at that. Somehow, word filtered back to Minnesota through Ann's siblings that this relationship sounded pretty serious, and during a weekend after spring break, Ann's mother decided to fly out to Seattle to see for herself. Would she disapprove?

Ann met her mother at the airport, and they drove to Ann's Queen Anne apartment, which looked deserted. After fifteen minutes, Ann said, "Let's go over to Capitol Hill. I can introduce you to Mike if he's home..." She and I had spent the previous day cleaning my apartment and removing any evidence of Ann McGrory living there. We hid her clothes, toiletries, and school books, feeling a little smug in disguising our secret so well.

Walking with her mom down the hallway of my apartment complex, Ann said, “Let’s check and see if he’s in,” knowing I was waiting for them. She rapped on the door, and I stalled for a minute before answering.

As Ann and her mother stood outside, they focused on the one bit of evidence we had somehow overlooked: “Ann McGrory,” posted prominently on the door alongside “Mike Nolan.” Ann didn’t say anything, but her mother smiled, pointed, and said, “I’ve heard a lot of nice things about him.” Maybe she was more progressive than we had given her credit for.

A couple weeks later, a frigate was brought into ship repair, just as Lee Vincent had predicted, but not everything went as planned. Vincent was moved over to a supervisory position at Yard One, another white hat took his place on the frigate, the crews in ship repair were reorganized, and I lost my “L”. It didn’t really matter, though. I only had two or three weeks to go in spring quarter; I could get through that, then get busy applying for school counseling jobs.

Although Ann and I were both in school and on target to finish the master’s program at the end of the quarter, we inhabited separate worlds, with Ann working during the day, and me working during the night. We saw one another midday at school, but the rest of the time we were like two meteors shooting across the night sky in different directions: I got off work and arrived home after Ann was fast asleep, and I slept in until just before class, long after Ann was up and gone.

Two different schedules meant we did almost all our serious talking on the weekend. Any question or concern or emotion was saved up for Saturday and Sunday, which sometimes made those two days intense instead of carefree.

There was a little greenbelt a block away from our apartment, a sloped grassy bank with a few trees and some benches. The greenbelt didn’t have a name, so Ann christened it “Nolan Park,” just one more sign of how intertwined our lives had become. It was an easy getaway for us, and we sometimes ate dinner there. I would pack a meal and a bottle of wine in a picnic basket; crystal glasses, cloth napkins—the works. We would dine at Nolan Park while enjoying the view: the Space Needle to the north, downtown Seattle in front of us, and the mountains to the south. It was the perfect place to watch a sunset. “I think you’re a romantic at heart,” Ann told me, which I found ironic, considering I was a late bloomer and unsure of myself exploring romantic relationships.

We spent hours in Nolan Park, and our long conversations made me appreciate how good Ann was for me. I wanted to be good for her, too. I loved being next to her, and sitting with my arm around her shoulder made me feel emotionally complete.

One spring evening found us on the park bench, balancing our picnic dinner and wine glasses on our knees while watching a pink-and-crimson sunset stretch over the city. It was one of those totally satisfying moments when people are content being silent together. We enjoyed our dinner and gazed at the pastel sky, and after a couple minutes I got the courage to say, "I think I'm falling in love with you." I had *shown* I was in love with Ann in a hundred little ways, but never said it.

Even though I was sure about my words, my heart swelled up to my throat as I said them out loud. The next step in our relationship was on the line, and I wanted to say something like "I'm being brave here, so don't trample on my heart."

Fortunately, Ann felt the same way I did. She waited a moment, then smiled and said the magic words. "I think I'm falling in love with you too."

I could breathe again. I poured more wine.

From that point on, I was a different person. Not in a way that other people would notice, but I was part of Ann and she was part of me. The relationship changed how I looked at some things, giving me a new frame of reference. At times it was like holding a mirror up to myself; when I shared opinions or views, I'd ask myself, *Do I honestly believe that?* Ann helped me expand the intellectual dimension of my life, as well as the emotional and physical dimensions. We married six months later.

At school, when spring quarter finally wrapped up, I wanted to get back on day shift so I could spend even more time with Ann. Putting in for a transfer, I was told to report to Yard One the following Monday, to work as a sandblaster on the modules for the next LSD. I wondered which scalers I would encounter in Yard One, thinking back to all the people I had worked with, and that made me remember Chris. My mind went over the good times we'd shared, starting with the two of us working overtime one weekend for Chief Black Cloud, getting drenched hosing down a passageway. I smiled as I pictured Chris clutching the fire hose, both of us exasperated and dripping wet. I thought of him driving us to work in his VW bus, drinking coffee while negotiating downtown traffic, the sound of his hand exerciser flexing in the background. With a shake of my head and a smile, my thoughts wandered from our "all you can eat" joints, to Chris wearing his blazer and tie for the opening day regatta, to the "zesty waiter" who always impressed the ladies and played spoons with the restaurant house band. *God …he was a great guy.* I missed my friend.

Monday morning I walked through the gate at Yard One, punched the time clock, and ambled over to the shipways, where giant steel modules were being assembled. I found the sandblasters' shed and was pleased to see a familiar face.

"Morning, L. T."

"Fine, and you?" was the instant reply. *Who else ever says that?* I nodded and shook his hand.

"Looking up, Nolan?" he asked.

"I'm looking up now, L. T." Grinning, I told myself, *There is only one L. T. McQuay in this world.* L. T. looked wiry and angular as always, not an ounce of fat on him. I could see that he still sported his "pocket knife"—half a hacksaw blade tied to a shoestring suspended from his belt loop.

"Been working hard?" I asked, already knowing the answer.

"Oh, I'm keeping up." L. T. grinned. "'Course, what Mother Nature and Father Time done took from me, I can't help, but I'm keeping up."

"I'll try to keep up with *you,*" I laughed.

"Well then, let's get to steppin.' You ever blast modules?"

"Some, but you can show me the finer points, like you did way back when, with me and the piss pot."

"Oh, I'm sure you've learned a lot since then." He winked and handed me a blasting hood. "All right, young man…"

The two of us were the sandblasting crew for the modules that would make up the next LSD. The best part of working on a crew that small was getting to know L. T. better, working with him closely. Among other things, I learned that L. T. used to run his own junk business, and he had plenty of stories about hauling away people's wrecked cars, broken refrigerators, and other assorted junk. Some of the stories involved jobs set up over the phone by White people who assumed that a guy named McQuay, someone with Scottish heritage, would be White. "I could tell I surprised a few people, but it didn't matter," L.T. laughed, "Black or White, junk is junk. It always got hauled and the job always got done."

I also learned that L. T. had worked on the side as a storefront preacher, and he still did. "Nolan, you should have seen me last weekend," L. T. said, shaking his head. "I was rollin' Sunday morning. I was preaching, *preaching hard*, and I could see people getting the fire in 'em, everybody moving and singing, you know, *catchin' hold of the spirit*. Then Little Sister"—one of L. T.'s granddaughters—"done got the holy spirit in her and raised up her hands and started shouting and dancing. *Praise the Lord!"* L. T.'s eyes sparkled as he put his arms up, shut his eyes, and swayed back and forth. It did me good to see L. T. so clearly pleased with himself.

Over the next two months, L. T. and I sandblasted the modules for the USS *Whidbey Island,* which was then assembled and launched from the Yard One shipways into the Duwamish Waterway. Tugboats ferried the vessel over to Yard Two for final assembly and outfitting, probably with Hildebrand as the scaler foreman.

A week after the *Whidbey Island* was launched, so was I, transferring to Yard Two to continue working aboard the *Whidbey Island*. Graduate school had ended, and I was busy filling out job applications.

The *Whidbey Island* reminded me of the AS39. I was aboard another mammoth Naval vessel in the middle stages of construction, grinding decks, fire watching, and prepping for painters. The difference was I'd be saying "so long" in a couple months, assuming I could land a school counseling job.

Other aspects of my life were changing. I brought Ann home one weekend, and at dinner we sat around a large table with the rest of my family. The conversation rolled along as it always did at home, plowing through the usual "Nolan" way of looking at things—assumptions I was brought up with, but never thought to challenge. My dad said something and everyone around the table nodded in agreement. Everyone but Ann.

With a smile on her face, Ann spoke up. "Really? I don't think of it like that." Although she spoke in the most positive way possible, conversation stopped as the faces around the table momentarily froze. Everyone nervously glanced between Dad and Ann, who went on to give her point of view. I was holding my breath, but when I looked at my dad, he was smiling.

"You know...you're probably right," Dad said, thoughtfully nodding, and the conversation got back on track. Everyone started talking again. With those few words, my dad had shown his openness and acceptance of Ann, and put everyone else at ease.

Reflecting that evening on what Ann had said, I thought, *You know, she's right. I agree with her.* I respected Ann's confidence in asserting herself and expressing her opinion. I admired her understated strength and the fact that she could go against the crowd in such a charming way. It made me love her even more. That insight, and the opportunity for me to grow because of it, became another compelling aspect of our relationship. Ann brought a new voice to my life, allowing me to examine—and sometimes challenge—my own long-held assumptions. She was opening windows for me, and I was invigorated by the fresh air pouring through and by the intriguing views.

My dad came to Seattle every so often to meet me for dinner. During my time in the shipyard, our relationship had grown beyond the father-son rapport I had grown up with. Now that I was on my own, we related to each other as adults—not only father and son but as two men who enjoyed each other's company. One weekend we were eating dinner at an Italian restaurant, and halfway through the meal, I asked, "Dad, how do you know when you've found the right person in your life?"

My father looked at me quizzically, so I added, "I'm in love with Ann. I know that much. But how can you be sure the person you love is *the* person? The right person…the one you want to spend the rest of your life with?"

He considered my question, then said, "Your heart tells you."

We sat in silence for a minute; Dad could tell I was thinking about what he had said. Then he broke the silence with "Tell me what you like best about Ann."

"Wow," I said, "there are a lot of 'bests' about Ann. For one thing, she's fun to be around." My feelings, of course, ran deeper than that, so I tried to describe how Ann made me feel complete, but found it was difficult to put into words. I said, "I admire her honesty, her compassion, and her sincerity. Believe it or not, one of the things I like the most is her ability to disagree with me and for us to have a conversation about the disagreement. I'm not used to that; normally that sort of conversation would just come to a polite halt for me. She respects my views, but she's self-assured enough to state her side of things. And she does it in a way that works. I like that. *I wish I could do that.*"

"I like those things about her, too," Dad said, smiling.

At home that evening, I thought about our conversation, especially Dad saying, "Your heart tells you." Even though it felt like jumping off a cliff, I knew my heart was telling me Ann McGrory *was* the person I wanted to spend the rest of my life with. Any indecision I felt earlier simply fell away as I told myself to follow Dad's advice and listen to my heart. Jumping off that cliff was the most natural thing I could do. Ann and I married shortly after that.

At this point I wasn't exactly sure when I would quit the shipyard, but I knew the end was near. I had to get a job offer first, and my confidence rose once I started lining up interviews. I missed work for the first couple meetings, then put in for a transfer back to swing shift so I could work at night and job hunt and interview during the day. The move ended up bringing me back to my sandblasting roots, working with my old buddies Eddie, Espy, Dunbar, and Richards.

I had crossed paths with Dunbar a couple times in the locker room, so I knew the guys were blasting on swing. I showed up on a Monday afternoon and was greeted by Eddie. "Yo, Brother Nols, what's happening?" Espy and Dunbar were there too, all blasting on the *Whidbey Island*, with Richards operating the sand pot, just like old times. Eddie asked, "You here to be our leadman again?"

I smiled and said, "Actually, I wondered if this crew needed a hose puller?" and everybody laughed.

Sandblasting with the guys took me back to old times. We were a team, and work felt familiar and comfortable. During that week I had two interviews scheduled: one on Tuesday and one on Wednesday. I never made it to the Wednesday interview. After driving home from the Tuesday meeting, I was met at the door by Ann.

"How did your interview go?"

"Good—I think—at least I came away with positive feelings."

"So you'd want to work there?"

"Sure."

"Good thing, because they called while you were driving back to offer you the job."

I shrugged my shoulders and grinned. "Okay…why don't I give them a call?"

On Thursday, a copy of a standard first-year school district contract arrived in the mail, along with a salary schedule. Holding the contract galvanized me, hope turning into reality. Then I laughed. "I've been 'Brother Nols' for five years," I told Ann. "Now students will call me 'Mister Nolan.' That'll take some getting used to."

"You can handle it."

I began reading the contract slowly as Ann looked over my shoulder and told me it looked exactly like the school contracts she had signed as a teacher. Then we looked at the salary schedule. Ann pointed to the top line, where first-year staff began: it had the lowest numbers. "You'll be starting right there."

"Wow—look at that!" I grinned with enthusiastic sarcasm, leaning closer, as though I couldn't believe the numbers; Ann could see I was smiling.

She shook her head. "You could keep working as a sandblaster…"

"No way." I straightened up. "This is my future. Besides, who in their right mind would pass up a deal like this?" The salary for a first-year counselor was $15,000, exactly *half* of what I was making as a leadman on swing shift. I held up the copy of my contract. "It's such a great deal!"

The humor was good for both of us. "Financially," I said, "this move is crazy. But I have managed to absorb enough wisdom from Nancy and from my dad to understand that money isn't the most important factor in the equation."

Ann put her hand on my shoulder, nodding her agreement. "It's important," she said, "but maybe not *most* important."

"I *have* to pursue something I love doing, a career I can grow in and, hopefully, become good at."

"It's the right path for you," she said.

Work at Lockheed that week felt surreal, like I was living on two different planets at the same time. Approaching one of the biggest crossroads in my life, I somehow expected the shipyard to be different, but it was just another day of work at Lockheed. Nothing here would change. I'd be gone, and everything else would continue on, the same as always. That made me feel disconnected, but it was balanced by unwavering confidence in my move.

Friday morning I called in sick and drove to the school district personnel office. Meeting with a secretary, I signed an official contract. "Welcome to the school district, Mr. Nolan." She beamed. "Here's your copy of the signed contract. We'll see you at the high school in three weeks."

"I'll be there." The numbers on the contract were indeed crazy—half pay!—but it made perfect sense to me. Young, happily married, and about to begin my career, I had come to the end of my second education. I was fulfilled.

I decided to make the following Friday my last day in the shipyard. I told the leadman, Harris, about my plans Monday afternoon and let the guys on the sandblasting crew know too. At the end of the shift Thursday night, Eddie stopped me and, taking me aside, said, "Bring something with you to drink tomorrow night."

"Okay…"

I walked into work Friday afternoon with a pint of Jack Daniel's in my lunch pail—not that I needed it; I was walking on air. Finally making my big career move was like watching myself star in a movie. That night we blasted a huge fuel tank, and as the shift wound down, we shut the hoses off a little early.

Once the sand settled and the air cleared, the guys brought out their liquor, and we set the bottles up in a line on a waist-high steel beam. Eddie had brought a little stack of Dixie cups from the locker room. "You don't walk far, to the sandblaster's bar!" Dunbar laughed.

"Cheers," Eddie said, pouring himself a drink.

After we had a couple, I turned to Eddie and, reaching into my pocket, handed him a small wooden wedge on a leather shoestring. "Time for me to give this back to you," I said. "Thanks for teaching me the tricks of the trade." Eddie grinned as he pocketed the wedge.

"Thanks for everything," I told him as I patted him on the shoulder.

Then I turned to the rest of the guys. "Thanks for making me part of the crew. You guys are great. Look at this," I said, pointing at the drinks, "even giving me a sendoff."

Eddie didn't say anything, but he raised his eyebrows in surprise. Dunbar started laughing.

"What sendoff?" Espy asked, chuckling with Dunbar.

"Oh, hell, Nolan," Eddie finally said. "We do this every Friday night when we blast on swing shift in ship repair."

Now I was the one laughing. "What the hell." I raised my Dixie cup. "Here's to sandblasting. Here's to you guys."

Dunbar raised his cup and added, "Here's to Brother Nols."

I shook hands with the guys and thanked them all again, especially Eddie. These were the men who got me here. I wish I could have put everything I felt into words, because I was saying goodbye to the "brother" part of Brother Nols, but I wasn't much of a speech maker, and it probably would have made the guys uncomfortable anyway.

We wrapped up, stowed our bottles, and headed off the ship. "You go get 'em, Nolan" and "You'll do fine, Brother Nols" echoed in my ears as I strolled down the gangway. Before I walked to the locker room, there was one more thing I had to do. I turned down the pier to the sand pot to say goodbye to Richards. My mentor—the sandblasting graybeard—was bent over the controls but straightened up as I approached. Our eyes met.

"So...you're the old sheep now, Nolan, the one who knows the road." He broke into laughter and shook my hand.

I damn near cried but managed to smile. With my throat tightening and my chin up, I pumped his hand. "It's time for me to go, Mr. Richards. Thanks for getting me here, for showing me the way. Thanks for everything."

As I shook his strong, calloused hand, Richards said, "You take care of yourself out there, Nolan, hear?"

I knew I would. *I knew I could.* I proved that much to myself here. Going forward, part of Lockheed Shipyard was going to stay with me, no matter what.

I was the last one to reach the locker room. After clearing out my locker, I sat on the wooden bench for a minute, staring at the sandblaster's hood in my hands, appreciating the moment. Then I hauled my gear down to the tool room. The whistle blew, and I got in the back of the line at the gate, ready to punch the clock one last time.

That final stamp on my timecard, at midnight, signaled I was through. I slowly walked through the parking lot, a little hesitant to let it all end. Drinking in the cool night air, I stopped and gazed up at the stars. I could hear L. T. McQuay asking, "Looking up?" Sandblasting didn't have anything to do with school counseling, but it had everything to do with me *becoming* a school counselor.

I would go on to a thirty-year career as a guidance counselor, work that I indeed loved, but I never lost sight of the fact that my confidence and sense of self were built on a solid foundation of sand. Lockheed Shipyard put the grit in me, and I'd always hold on tight to that.

I watched the last few cars zoom off into the cool night, the sounds of their engines eventually fading, and all of a sudden I was surrounded in silence. A beautiful silence. Alone in the parking lot, I looked up to the stars, and everything felt perfect. I said aloud, "Okay, Mister Guidance Counselor, let's get to steppin'."

Further Reading

For further reading about the Ship Scalers Union in Seattle, I recommend two University of Washington research papers, available online through UW Libraries' ResearchWorks:

- "'There Were Years of Neglect': The Ship Scalers Union and Seattle's Racial Progressivism in the 20th Century," by Adam Farley, 2011 (http://hdl.handle.net/1773/16592)
- "The Whacking of Ship Scalers Local 541," by Peter Costantini, 2018 (http://hdl.handle.net/1773/41648)

Acknowledgements

Thank you Nancy, Cathy, Tricia and John: family members always encouraging me and uplifting my writing.

Thank you to my editor, Kirstin Andrews of Kite String Editing, traveling with me on this journey from start to finish.

Thanks to the good folks at Washington State University Press for believing in my story and bringing my book to publication, especially Linda Bathgate and Caryn Lawton.

Thank you to individuals who provided much needed support in the early stages of the book: Tim Roos, John Brewer, and John Eekhoff. Thanks also to Linda, Gordy, Sheri, Rosemary, Mary Ann, and my other fellow writers at the Port Angeles Senior Center Writers Group, for their help and encouragement over the years.

Special thanks to John Gallagher for his friendship and enthusiastic support throughout the storytelling process.

And thank you to writers Jonathan Evison, Thomas Kohnstamm, and Tony Tekaroniake Evans for their literary insights and guidance.

About the Author

A native Washingtonian, Mike Nolan has worked as a dishwasher, a short-order cook, a sandblaster, a counselor, and a professional clam digger. After a thirty-year career as a guidance counselor in the public schools, he graduated and is now working as a writer. Mike and his wife Ann live in Port Angeles, Washington, where the Olympic Mountains meet the shores of the Strait of Juan de Fuca.

Photograph credit: *Shari Fultz Photography.*